Double Feature!

Just Call Me Mom

The Purple Bathrobe

M. J. Scott

Copyright 2018

Daniel Wetta Publishing

Other Books by M. J. Scott:

Journey into Fulfillment

Time on the Turn

Power Steering

Power Steering 2

Sport's Alien Fantasy (Co-author Daniel Wetta)

Visit Author Website: www.danielwetta.com/powersteeringus/

DEDICATION

I take this opportunity to dedicate this book with great appreciation to all the institutions of learning that have been my privilege to serve. In all the classrooms across the country that have been filled with children, I loved them then and now! To the professional organizations that have broadened my scope of teaching and learning skills, you have my sincere gratitude.

I believe that angels do walk the earth. So, to this world providing angels who noted my love for writing inspirational messages, I commit this work with deep and humble gratefulness for the spiritual guidance provided along the many roads traveled. My angels have been my closest friends and publisher, and if my words lift others, then my mission is accomplished.

Thanks, family, friends and readers!

With love,

M. J. Scott, USA

Table of Contents

Just Call Me Mom

One

Joining the sorority of moms with its huge population really begins with the Garden of Eden in the pages of sacred history. To achieve this status, we must first give recognition to the presence of the chosen team member. The borrowed rib provided the strength for generations then and the mystical creation reaching NOW!

There's a sisterhood that can be found worn on the faces of Moms around the world. Look in the eyes of all ages of women from the silent singles to the grandmothers walking alongside (if by good fortune.) The page of recognition for their achievements is blank, awaiting the intuitive entries that bond one to another in society.

Today is a Sunday of early rising moments, and it, too, will produce its own path of direction. Heartbeats are measurable units expressing what it means to be a Mom for the joy that is immeasurable. The sisters of sorority walk to the inner beats of music when love is in the masterpiece. Just for now the word, "responsibility," rings clear.

Two

Lift this bundle of enchantment and shower it with the tender compassion that is the willing promise of moms (and dads) for the future of the world! Don't allow the clouds of generational space to separate these moments, because connections provide leadership and understanding. Allow the flow of generational love. This is the unique passage through the doorway of blessings. The pouring of lifelong companionship is a powerful gift from Mom or Dad as a boost for the growing little ones to overcome life's hurdles, big and small.

Should we urge giving advice, or should we be silent and allow natural want and need to open this door of communication? As the years beckon in the silence of living away from the din of noise, Mom reaches out and says, "I love you!" The umbilical connection is stronger than ever. This is the very essence of MOM. It is apparent in the softness of a tear moistening the cheek. Mom knows what is correct.

In past cultures, the teaching of the gentleness of love and the power of compassion was not expressed in the world. These amazing teachings were buried and plowed into ruts deeper and deeper with no recognition of the trusted truths to share.

Leaving this page to rest in the thought of what might have been, we move forward to the edges of destiny to pursue purpose. This is a little step towards "momism."

Three

There's a "momism" that blossoms even when some moms are ready to fall off their chairs in exhaustion. In walking through the living room with the audio on mute, there stands a banner note: "An 'app' now for Moms to connect!"

Wow, is that intuitive telepathy or just a dire need to encourage the cycle of raising the family?

There are many titles that fit into the space of "mom." Let's see... Mrs. Mom, Ms. Mom, Mr. Mom, Grand Mom and even Pop, too. These days children are generous in their reports of "What did you do at school today?" However, the germ population isn't mentioned until the second day of school arrives, a day too late! Grandpa comes to school to visit and gets a virus. Grandma gets the stomach flu. Everyone looks surprised! Now, instead of wearing shoes into the house or apartment when coming in from the garage, try taking off those germ collectors and put on a pair of slippers. The shoes may have had some not-so-rare encounters with the germ and virus population that tracks around silently. My goodness, I don't wear hats, but mentally wear the hat of remembrance of the Asian custom of slippers at the threshold, entry hall or landing. This makes a softer entry into the home, and even voices become a little gentler.

Let's watch the first set of shoppers at the fabric store. There's the blonde, tired-looking Mom with her two-year-old-look-alike in the shopping cart. Then we spot the first grader who keeps bringing Mom ideas of personal gifts in an early Christmas season. She gently says, "Take it back, and if you are very good, I'll think about it!" That lasts about three minutes until the swift eyes and hands land upon another object. This time, it is a well-designed stick animal in a carry along cage. Mom looks exasperated and says, "What did I tell you?" The glum face runs off with a pout, and sister dear is now throwing her toy on the floor. Oh, you say you have seen this all before! Yes, and Mom is still trying to thumb through the pages of a dress-designer catalog and will hopefully find a fabric to match her desires. By this time, sister precious is putting the toy in her mouth and brother precious is pulling on Mom's dress for attention, too. At last to the rescue, here comes Grandmom! Observe that now there are three look-alikes of females in a row and a resembling boy. The women could have been three-generation-triplets. The only difference is that Grandmom is smiling, and you can read her thoughts: "I was there once like you are now, dear!"

This is fun! Let us go shopping in the mall to find more "momism!"

Four

A pretty sports car just drove up, painted in a new blue, and the couple are carrying blue grocery bags. This suggests that the refrigerator is about to be fed. They aren't into the family way, but there's potential, so if they want an introduction into this field of study, we just may have hit on a hot item. "Beware This May Create an Awakening!"

Just a closing note from the view into the ocean blue and the pearl shades of sky. "Thank you, Lord, for protecting so many from the ravages of the recent hurricane's rage. Bring water, food and shelter

for those who are returning through the highways of disaster."
Mother Earth has suffered too!

Here's a lift of powdered sugar being blown from the hands of a baking-cupcake-woman. The advertisement executives missed this blooper. It happened so eye-blinking swiftly. Moms should be added to the watch teams.

Five

MOM'S APPLE PIE deserves its very own homemade-pie crust. It was just learned that introducing this storybook title has at least three generations involved. The apple pie season has arrived, and fresh apples flow in daily from the orchards. Deciding the apple-taste variety is strictly your own choice, but how these are prepared has its own design. Now the apple-crunch topping must become the open-faced pie with brown sugar and crumbs that melt into the vanilla homemade ice cream. The old churn plunged into the ice in the big metal tub always awaits the kids to operate. The crust is another task with a recipe of flour and shortening followed by a knife cutting it up into crumbs. The wad gets made, and here comes the rolling pin.

For three generations, all the pies have been predominately open-faced. That's just the way they are made. Mouth-watering goodness emits from the oven in aroma of dreamy dessert. Not until Grandma's pies and Mom's pies reached the granddaughter's kitchen did this exclamation sound, "Do you mean pies have top crusts?" Great laughter fills the kitchen at the thought of pumpkin pies with lids. Cream pies only come with whipped cream. How did the world ever manage to ruin pies with hats? If there was a tradition established, it has been lost now in the grocery freezer section. Even key lime pie has refused a crusty top. In serious thought, perhaps the top of pie became a pie shell after the Puritan sacrifice of ocean crossing.

Tomorrow, the Gala, Grimes Golden and Macintosh apples will have a visitor intent on sliced-pie fixings or apple sauce for this time-of-year indulgence. Thanks, Mom! Then in the artsy design, a lattice of crust will allow the apples to peek through. Apple -blossom season bursting into pie season and Thanksgiving, too! Go ahead and learn the true story about Johnny Appleseed when his love died. To remember her, he planted apple seeds all over the Midwest. There are still monuments to Johnny's trees throughout the United States. For romanticism, let's say the Shenandoah Valley is his home, too.

Six

There is a gentle radiance when the day closes that reminds us of St. Benedict's quote, "Always we begin again!" This feels so right in the tomorrow that we create through the best we have to offer. Suddenly, the clouds part and allow an accent of sunlight. We look towards the West, and the thought hits us: Mom is on duty 24-7. St. Benedict's encouragement of renewal reminds us of Mom's commitment day after day.

Time-out to jump into the shower and streak to the bathroom scales! Taking a load off the feet planted firmly beneath the keyboard of delight. Reading the emails connects us in special ways with other writers. One just shared her Momism joy of taking her daughters out for their birthday celebrations at an Asian restaurant and then off to bowling. Her joy radiated through the story of the heavy bowling ball that created a disclaimer and was put back on the rack. The laughter about gutter balls spilled from her electronic message. Now she and the girls are off to become authorities on the Revolution from a visit to the Yorktown museum. I note her goal and rejoice in my circle of friends.

The next e-mail memory is set in the kitchen of Grandpa Chef, who was attending his culinary details. He had just bidden farewell to his grandchildren after a quick stop over, but it was the one-year-old great-kid who had consumed him. It seems that this born atom of energy was one that Grandpa said could take on Isis. Now that is a mouthful without many other details! Did anyone sleep that night of the big stay-over? Try writing! Even little paragraphs allow

7

thought admissions that for their readers become billboards without autographs.

If you are wondering why this author seems to be borrowing others' family stories, there's a big reason. My two families have successful and creative careers, and my daughters and sons-in-law didn't have time for delivery-room take-outs. So, this Mom has never questioned this omission. Admittedly, it would have been difficult to scuba dive with an extra carry-on or to make the visits to the museums across the continent and direct the plays associated with their programs. Yes, they do have very full lives of love, happiness and sharing when the moments speak. So, if you are in similar position, do the same as me: adopt the joys of watching others' wee tikes grow. It's a big and fulfilling surrogate's role.

Seven

"Good morning!" brings a surprise anecdote to rising blueness. So, dear Moms, if your computer screen has been filling up, try going back and checking what's important! Hit the proper key again and make a sizeable deposit to the glass at the bottom of the screen. As you save the important entries, print out a few just for reading in daylight. The blue cartridge gets a new look. Isn't it amazing what a new cartridge can bring to the day? New thoughts rise, then the pink one says, "I'm ready for breakfast too!" So, with the printer having had a big impact on getting the day organized, we are off to a fresh start. Pink and blue are little baby-size colors that line nursery windows. Sometimes, when colors spring out of the unexpected, we should take another look at the cup of blessings and record them. Winging moments are now positive and colorful. Don't forget to put your slippers on to complete the soft accompanying feeling.

Eight

This is a gentle entry into a secret hidden cove of Mom's private wealth. With your encroaching curiosity, you will mine for gold without picks and shovels. As you enter the silent treasure of the female mind, your alertness becomes keen in this daring journey.

Within this venture, you may experience the sensation of blindness, or you might painstakingly move through fog and mist in which tears find rest. The slow necessity of step-by-step forces work to be pushed aside. You discover an oasis of retreat. In the light layers of dreams, you find yourself floating in channels inside a hope-filled building.

All is still. Only the eyelashes make a little flicker of movement. There are no hammers and drills noisily disrupting this mecca of unspoken language. Great reservoirs of learning through experience have been stored, resources for the classes from preschool and beyond. The accumulation is boxed, contents not shredded, all prepared through the strength of personality and courage. The original sources are traced through lines of heredity hidden until blood types are snatched.

Fascinated? Note your thoughts as you explore this community of inherited learning rarely acknowledged. Great sensitivity becomes a testing ground where endurance provides strength. Moms will probably not laugh when the offspring chime, "Are we there yet?" Their inner preparation and intuition naturally hold the fort for this and similar questions through the years.

The evolutionary talents and skills of the female gender easily prepare moms to write the novels yet unwritten, based on an infinity of experiences. But, equally, moms who are veterans of construction of childhood projects can move on to create engineering marvels. Bubbling with energy, moms ignite smiles into laughter, and the miracle of family love suggests mystery that hides more. They think occasionally about untouchable, secret loves that were sacrificed so that contentment and stability continue. The memories may remain asleep until a distant future when the lover's kiss arrives.

A tear just escaped!

Nine

The sensitive heart beats a pulse unmeasured but enduring. Its erratic fluctuations make themselves known through the occasional heartbreaks.

Moms absorb those times in silence. They yearn for that power nap so often denied or even given a thought. You don't have to wear a nametag for this to reach your filtering understanding. You recognize it. Let's give this organ a prominent place to share in the glow and joy of happiness. You have heard of the blue bloods where some hierarchy was given introduction. In the arena of the red bloods, everyone documented in life knows the voices of reality. Everyone holds these experiences in his or her hearts and can allow excitement to radiate or apply a little blush of surprise.

Motherhood fulfills destiny that is personal and mysterious. If you feel this excitement, then you have joined this tour of life in its orbiting seconds.

"Are we there yet?"

Ten

Winging thoughts were just passed in the speed of light by a pair of gold finches in their own splendor. The bluebirds haven't graced sight yet today, but they will come and perform their daring dances. Just for a moment more, allow these romantic and poetic witnesses to add luster to a cloudy day. Turn up the rhythms of music and become one with this harmony that can include you. So often we think that harmony is something on the bookshelves, something purchased and written long ago. No prescriptions will ever provide the ecstasy of the soul that touches the finches' wings.

Soul has its own silent wave lengths, and this unsolved mystery will never be reached through intrusion by artificial intelligence. Prayer will be the petition of protection, and the "Master of the House" will answer with the whole of heaven applauding.

Dancing sunlight reflections will hold promise, and the golden sunbeams will encase themselves in memory's keeping.

Eleven

This computer screen had been left open, and a sender gave word of safety after the storm. Now the news is shared in *Just Call Me Mom!* Now, in relief, learning can move ahead.

In a recent interview on a game show, a contestant shared that he was an educational researcher. But he had a lifetime of viewing and listening to help assimilate his professional training. He is presently working with a newborn in a bilingual, English and Spanish family. How does the child learn? No present books reveal what the researcher will discover. Fascination with this research will invite our interest too.

A philosophy professor said in a class of logic, "There's nothing new under the sun!" May I disagree, however? With great respect, he was a gifted man of theology, and he opened the doors to our potential thinking abilities. He always held heaven on the edge of his lips. Personal: He laughed and told me once, "You have been given a B, because you have a long way to go!" Was he a Seer or a Seeker?

Twelve

Just fourteen minutes ago, this screen was left in silence. That was time enough for a shower and catching the hot water without being burned. The phone rang, and then I sat to listen to the anguish of a precious friend facing a serious guilt trip!

I am not invading privacy to reveal that her aging mother has serious issues of needing 24/7 care. My dear friend shared her mountain of worries. Wanting to help resolve some resulted in my reminding her to put her own health first, for her large family depends on her for care, too. Her husband, returning from a business trip, calls often the mother-in-law, which is a support to his wife. He provides that pillar of strength so needed!

Within our conversation, I shared that I had this book in construction. She is my young guiding angel who has reintroduced me to life, publishing and deep friendship. She shared that her mother is in a rehab facility and in sound mind, demanding to return to the home of her daughter and son-in-law. Listening, I noticed that she did not realize that for her, the bathroom is her seat of security rather than the housecoat worn in her own private suite.

Digital calling, sharing, and now her husband is waiting at the train station to return this evening. Right time! Right place!

Thirteen

A powerful word just came dashing across the email like a jet stream. My goodness, "restoration" arrives silently in memory links to past experiences. If only these experiences were all packaged in a tin can, so they couldn't go out to contaminate! These sharp ragged attacks have been borne through the years from people trying to control the listening ears.

So, never fall prey to these: To a child in a state of disbelief in learning that her eyes were green by her mother saying, "You have snake eyes!" Well, that must have been a colorful memory. Another adult fragment of hate: "I don't want to ever see you again!" Or, in a closing marriage, someone tells the departing one, "I'll treat you like garbage if I want too!" That poor soul receiving disparaging rage didn't walk away in any condition except deep, dredging hurt. More shocking statements that are heard don't need to be divulged today. Restoration is a wonderful thing when getting a loose bumper repaired or having other little bumps fixed on the memory wagon. There's much more, yes, but restoration occurs when we do not internalize personally the attacks on our souls.

Just a little tap on the shoulder from Mom!

Fourteen

These eyes had a windshield view along this road of life on yesterday's adventure. Four wheels running when a sturdy auto stream provided words to stimulate. The license plate ahead held no rust. "8 GIRLS," it proclaimed, and the car also had a big emblem for Ohio State University. Also, in tiny little words on the plate of discovery was the urge to "Eradicate Autism!" This vehicle of movement just spelled out a wonderful traveling story. The lady driving was diminutive, and her countenance remained secluded as she turned at the next stoplight. It was a story of vibrant life, energy and love in boundless measure!

Then the blinking message light on my phone was the next encounter: "Please call me right back!" I dialed quickly and found that the request came with a surprise. The postal card I had received a week before, which just couldn't be thrown away (for no reason except the intuitive said, "Save!") was an inquiry whether I was interested in selling my house.

Just call me sensitive even to the errands of trucking out the trash. Don't choke on this entry hidden in a cart with wheels. So, wheeling along, I went outside, and an out-of-state car drove into a space I was passing. I turned and said, "Hi, New York!" The young lady got out with a big smile, and we shook hands. If I had been carrying the bag of contents instead of wheeling, that might have hindered our chance meeting. She has a beautiful name and a coveted position in the design industry. Life is filled with little stories that make me wonder why writers feel they have hit a block and lack stimulation. What to write is always around us, sometimes hidden in ultra-small moments.

Next, I admired a handsome young man standing on a residential street corner as he tapped a number on his cellular phone. Quickening thoughts of how far his voice would travel! The content is his own secret.

Don't ignore chance encounters that seem like small things. If we view life as one moment at a time, then the stories assembled sum to blessings. As for me in this moment, today holds a question of, "What is to be worn on the Monday of jury duty? Should it be resort casual?"

Fifteen

Dear children, have you ever asked what unspoken thoughts that parents could reveal? This morning of autumn blessings, the sun is sprinkling glistening droplets. The dew has returned to sparkle like diamonds that were never mined from the soil. Silent parental gifts of the mind reach out beyond the rules for living. Think of them as your great partners in this journey of life.

We all share in this school of life, but did anyone ever teach us how to be parents beyond the boundaries of a lecture? Wherever we are on this yardstick of life, it's a wonderful inch-by-inch experience.

Take a moment after foraging through your bowls of energy bars to find a renewing set of values. These are absorbed without pressure. Each culture has its own structure for this. "Respect" and "responsibility" are elusive words with great expectations.

How are respect and responsibility taught? These are important. They form a lining of strength to make the world a better place. Catalogs and designs are not available for the weave of this wonderful lining of love. There are many kinds of love to nurture you, and all form the very personal and private you. Searching for this flow is exciting and challenging. Welcome to life and love!

Sixteen

Wash your face, clean your teeth and dress for the soul search that is asking to be given open space. This isn't any wrestling match; rather, it's a creative path though the vineyards of harvest. Today, we will work our way into a vineyard to breathe the refreshing aroma of ripening fruit on trestles of flavors. Clusters to become masterpieces. Drenching ourselves in this moment of unbottled liquid for the first time feels like a baptism for the soul in wine of ageless years.

Where did this stimulating plan begin? It may have been yesterday when placemats were found and purchased for the family table. The pictures imprinted on the placemats with wine and roses lured my soul.

Time Out! I'm getting dressed for a close-by or a distant journey. I haven't decided. Let's check the navigation system beside the steering wheel. Perhaps it will lead to another entry in *Power Steering 3.*

Seventeen

Dear Moms, this is a little undocumented type of diet that could provide you a mellow feeling. This diet isn't advertised on any channels. It comes from the harvesting of Turas. These little songs have melodies that have filtered the storms of life and ride on the winds from the shores of some highland unnamed and freely sung. Trua-Tru-La...it's like Do-Re-Me...that expresses the freedom of soul being. The diet is taking time to rejuvenate your body, mind and soul. This requires only your willingness to provide yourself with a sustainable energy source for continuing in your commission as a Mom. Try sharing the resource with Mr. Dad for an added blend of intimacy. Add in the power of spirit from heaven's resource reservoir.

Restoration of time takes the (die) out of "diet." Have you figured out what's important? The store-purchased diets or your own leisure resting on a song? Perhaps, a little children's book called, "A Basket of Songs" bursts forth into printed artistic picture-and-word expression. You have inspired me to unpack a box from the days, weeks, months and years of hidden storage. Thank you!

Eighteen

Dear ones, we all get mixed signals at times. On my computer, I was just the recipient of "This manuscript is being locked."

However, going to another intersection of computer files allowed access to continue.

I'm so glad, because while watching the clustering clouds and changing some afternoon plans, the sun broke through, and the ultraviolet rays changed the tree tops into a burnished copper dressing. It was so dramatic that not even the camera had time to gasp, "Wait for me!" These little transformations are fascinating and so often left unrecorded. I'm guilty too! Our lives are a color pallet for our creations.

This afternoon is an open book, but not next week with its calendar offering a difficult juror's straight chair. So, the approaching rays of afternoon today allow for a cup of tea and choice of seating. A water view would be refreshing, and a vineyard is still calling. We'll have to check the weather and camera for agreement. The lighting exposures must be perfect. How I am enjoying the steam rising above the china teacup! There's a chair waiting if you care to join me.

Nineteen

Excuse the interruption when I dashed away thirteen minutes ago. That can be a lucky number, also. Perhaps running on fumes is my confession to explain the power nap I took.

The beginning of the millennium was begun with great anticipation. Along in August, there came a stormy emotional warning that colon cancer surgery was just days away. Now, this was serious, as I had just signed a once-in-a-life time teaching position with a Christian Academy. So, with all accelerators pressed to the gas pedal, I made a pact with the "Master of the House." Yes, that's the Lord who holds the great permission in charge of destiny. I said, "Okay, Lord, if you pull me through this, I'll make a vow to write again and, finally, listen to your long-ago calling." The gifted specialists told me, "You have a 55% chance, and I took those odds without any hesitation. Then came four chemo treatments, and I said, "That's it!" They said, "You have to take six weeks to recover," but the determined M.J. said, "No, I have an obligation to my new students, and I'll be there in three weeks."

Now, I know you are either shaking your head in disbelief or believing in miracles. There have been interludes in which the pen or keyboard have been neglected, but now its full steam ahead! The cup of tea is still waiting somewhere, and since there isn't anyone who chose to join me, I'm back at the keyboard enjoying the circle of golden friendship and a touch of heaven. Just call me, "Mom." There's power in prayer and miracles!

Twenty

Let's be a little reckless and brush up the carpet and give it a new look. Then, to add to these few quarantine moments, splash the coffee table with some mirror-like face lift. The dishwasher should be almost done, and the washing cycles finished. Folding up the housekeeping issues can be followed by the glorious lift of the windows to let in the fresh breezes. Now, if you would write down your mirthful thoughts, we have accomplished a new line of credit. It's so much fun to make miniscule ideas that cause a little chuckle. Then, teaching the kids how to get these little jobs done in record order, don't offer them pennies, dimes or quarters, but say, "Let's go for a walk or shopping, or have our own little tea party! The fresh tablecloth is an announcement of a wholesome contribution, too.

Afterwards, the conversations can stem around what will be fun to do together the next time we have the house ready for company. If a chiming of "making cookies" is the recipe for precious time together, then, sure enough, that is the winner. Out comes the calendar, and we mark this party time as an appointment to be kept.

Having things to look forward to is like free tickets to a circus. Little tickets can be made out by the kids of what they will contribute. These are work incentives that build responsibility. Someone oversees finding the recipe for which all agree. Check the cupboard for ingredients and make a shopping list. Well done! If there are two or three little exercises in preparation, that's wonderful. If desirable, invite the Auntie to come and provide a helping hand through a guest performance with her "home economics" experience.

See, having kidlets around can be such a joy! A little tradition at our house has always been that the living room will always be ready for company at the end of the day. So, the toys are placed in their own little guarded habitats. One last thought as they are tucked into the waiting, freshly made beds: In the morning, the bed must be made. See who has the best wrinkle-free look.

Oh, I liked the word, "kidlets," but you won't find it in the dictionary of etiquette. Just call me mom. I'm exercising my license for being vocabulary bold and encouraging quick thinking about the needs of others. Is there a smiley face available?

Twenty-One

Where goes the night when yesterday's thoughts linger? Is it the toss-and-turn or the eyes-wide-open walk right out of that den? We all have skeletons from the past that were buried and about which we don't talk.

In the joys of searching the closet for photography enlargements of nature's beauty, I discovered an unrecognized leather portfolio springing from the past, so unannounced. The shock was a seismic wave, and it had to be stopped abruptly. Now, in the middle hours of night, how do I dispose of this remnant? The former owner is no longer in this physical world, and yet memory-clouds swirl with smoke signals of abuse. Should this be placed in a box and shipped off to the heirs? This will take a brave heart to even touch the package and mail. A tiny baby shoe was lurking inside those pages, and another mother had cherished it! So, with respect for the woman who had beautiful, silky, silver hair, it will be shipped to her next-born.

The jury duty was cancelled, and in those calendar-saved hours, the leather folder was placed in the mail and the verdict was not guilty. Those moments in determining what to do with that package from destiny has been like falling down the stairs and breaking ribs. Not even able to call for help as there was no breath! Sometimes even masking tape won't be a remedy.

Wonderful, a closet hurdle will be crossed on Monday. Just another marathon that has been won. There's an email provider that would understand! No charges, just postage. This juror has answered and checked off the summons and left the court house of duties.

Sometimes, *Just Call Me Mom* holds unexpected responsibilities and continual growth.

Twenty-Two

As today edges closer to the after-five reminiscing, I have trouble in spelling correctness. The tally today will soon show up as being a day filled with bloopers!

First, determining that yesterday's discovery of destiny baby boot must be mailed today! Even the accompanying pictures and yellowing news clips had to go! So, on the way to the post office with ample time for the 10:30 appointment, the well-traveled street needs a "Deer Crossing" sign posted. Out of the forest and right in front of my white bumper came this leaping, mid-grown young buck. He was traveling at a galloping speed, and my 30 mph was meant to swerve right, and he raced on to the left. We didn't meet.

The next odd thing was that the postal service parking lot wasn't very well populated. I had a hasty thought, "This is luck!" Inside, the sign posted read, "10:00 a.m.: New Saturday hours." Should I wait twenty-seven minutes or forget this demanding duty? Another option was to try the Fed Express office in the little mall. At their door came the sign, "I'll return in ten minutes!" Now, if frustration needed a second cup of coffee, this certainly registered. But soon a hefty hand produced a key and unlocked the office for meeting my needs. He carefully packaged the portfolio, and the charge was met with a ten-dollar bill to travel in one business day about fifty miles.

However, this is the weekend. So, dials were required from sender to receiver, because it had been forgotten that the express company didn't accept post office box addresses. They need a physical address! Well, that was my blooper!

After that, the day moved smoothly until deciding where to have lunch. Homeward-bound seemed to be the best solution. After a short twenty-minute power nap, the adventure of heading out to find a luxurious tea setting on a patio at the winery caught my focus. Of course, the camera was neatly stowed in my purse and safely tucked in a slip-on case from an Outer Banks visit in North Carolina. The cushioned kind! Now, memory took the wheel, and the road moved from wide to narrow and came to a dead end. Turning around was not a problem, and this allowed me to see these gorgeous residential homes, like castles, overlooking a not-visible river. The grape vines were looking empty, so I made a stop and took a long camera shot atop an embankment. White, fluffy clouds seemed to be laughing. Then, "lost" was my next realization. A nice man drove up and got out, and the result for my inquiry was, "Get some good directions to the Winery." Plus, he added, "They picked the grapes last week!"

Twenty-Three

He didn't smile, even when he was wearing his old alma mater sweat shirt. I introduced myself as an author and photographer and wanted to get to the Winery. He said, "Take this next right turn, keep going to the next right turn, and take one more."

But in following his directions, I discovered that he had directed me back to the main highway.

That's okay, when this blooper is deposited, I'll check the directions on the computer and try again. Just so happy that I didn't have a guest that earlier was invited. It would have been a trip to somewhere and going nowhere.

No problem, I'll drive downtown to the post office and pick up the mail. On the way, with traffic behind me, a man with intent not to stop drove right out and made his left turn in front of me. Oh well, this is blooper day. Then it became noticeable that nowhere in this excursion had I seen any children out playing. We do have a sizeable school budget, but today the children were existing inside their home four walls. When I passed the church entrance, a young couple came out holding a tiny infant who was, maybe, just a few weeks old. At last, a set of parents and a baby too!

The post office parking lot was the only one in town not packed. Even the stoplights were sluggish, but waiting was okay. A chocolate frosty would have been the next temptation, but, instead, the green bill got thrown in the map case. I had the thought I have every time: "I don't indulge. The map case can digest it without calories."

The day of bloopers eased into music filling my home with rhythms that will be enjoyed, so I brought a cup of coffee to the patio. The flowers and second growth of tomatoes won't mind my company. When you have a day showcased with bloopers, there is still one remaining: I forgot to tell you that at the checkout stand at a store, a young college student asked, "Would you like to contribute to The Katrina Fund?" Somewhere she wasn't instructed to say "Irma!"

Just call me mom. I've been blessed again: Sunday, church, and dinner out with the family. Thanks for keeping my day from a total blooper!

Twenty-Four

Dear Readers, there's a sea of descriptions, encryptions, instructions and numbers, and it's all caught up in some mystical cloud hanging over my head. I can deal with getting the car inspected and the new Department of Motor Vehicles decals that just arrived. Now, what to do with just trying to get into the computer for driving directions? I'm a good listener in getting directions, but, please, must there always be passwords to climb over or, worse yet, to remember? That's it! I'll get a hard-copy map if these are still in print! I belong to AAA, that's the auto kind! They smile when I get the concierge assistance. Been there, done that, too!

Thank goodness, my editor has the patience of Job, and that's the biblical one! If this can be designated to his desk of editing worries, my early morning dilemma will reside in the outgoing basket. Just let me write, dream and feel the joy and freedom right here at any time of day! Shake your head up or down - at least this crept into your acknowledgement. Even the spell check is kind when these fingers don't match the straight-line brain waves to the keyboard. One finger missed a letter, and it turned into rain. Oops, that made for an allergic sneeze. At 3:30 a. m., there's still hope for a little comedy to strengthen the last tissue!

There are stand-up billboards all over town advertising, "Get your Flu Shot Here!"

Maybe a skydiver or flying billboard could advertise, "Get your laugh from *Just Call Me Mom*." It would never designate which mom. Safety in numbers!

Which password will get into the vault, and it forgot to ask, "What's your country of origin?" Smile, we're all just kids at heart, but please don't let me stumble while racing to catch the airplane waiting for me, like once in Tokyo. "All Aboard!" The day ahead is exciting when there are no plans, maps or directions. There is an open ticket to return!

Twenty-Five

Spin your chair 360 degrees and return in seconds from being lost. How can we dash away when the music is swelling up to the cathedral ceiling in gentle sound waves? "The Sound of Music" is encrypted into my brain waves and lets the moments burst forth with JOY. Oh, to share that these angelic gifts of microseconds can soothe the very soul of each of us! Now, unbend the body, straighten, and go place your head against a welcoming pillow. Moments have reached that relaxation for the mind and soul. Streams of happiness within.

From the wheels of sound penetrating through the distance come an entry that is reaching out from beyond. The train was following its tracks toward a destination which we really don't care to follow. There's another following reminder from the heart which is wonderful. We recognize the physical pounding of the heart and the gentle smooth breathing of the lungs, but when the spirit of soul calls our attention, what do we do?

From the closed eyes that refuse to dwell in the zone of deep sleep comes a dimension that we often fail to proclaim aloud. There's no backtracking if we refuse to let it speak. It's not frightening or fearful in that wavelength gifted from the heavens above into the heaven within. We glance at the screen and are relieved that it hasn't found the dungeon of loss.

There's a sweeping of the clock hands that really doesn't need to record the actions of this blissful moment. This pouring of faith has been given a flow that warms even our cold feet. We feel warm and have the feeling of treading on sacred ground. The mind of man has many plans, but the purpose of God is established. In these moments, the quilt of comfort has found a new sensitivity to life. There is an indwelling love that allows the orbits to remain in their own spinning significance. And to us of earth-bound awareness, it is love that makes life so filled with the giving, the sharing and the purpose for which we all were created.

Bowing to the Sunday of reverence: Do we answer this call? Answering the call can be shown in turning on the printer, powering up and sharing from the heart of caring.

Swallow, and return to your first morning sip of nourishment. Java for me! "Oh, thank you, Master of the House!" Saved by Grace! A chill, and I'm going back to catch a power nap.

Twenty-Six

Windows allow the morning to pour forth its light. In the distance, a converging view is witness to the thin veils of white clouds that finger a rising fog above the sea. Watching, I see that the clouds are

23

moving gently from west to the eastern shore. Next, the east begins to speak, as there are rushing dark clouds of a hurricane named Jose that is off the shore line. How far it reaches out or inland is beyond our eyes to yet perceive.

Families are a precious focus today! This morning, a family of five walked up the walkway and found chairs waiting for them here in church. Dad was carrying one big bag; Mom sported a backpack; and the youngsters were ready to unpack and get on with the expedition. But there was not a peep of noise. The littlest child laid her soft fold-up book on her mother's lap and began to read. When a little word came out, Momma touched her lips. Silence continued in this enjoyable moment. The other two children occupied themselves busily while Dad kept an eye on the pick-up-and-put-away stuff. It was a family project, and when the "Children's Story Time" invitation arrived, Mom and the three little musketeers trotted up to the front of the sanctuary. The pastor's story time was filled with delight and silence. Then she invited them to follow her, armed with a bag of yellow popcorn. Dad saw their exodus and picked up the remaining treasures and joined the others down the corridor.

For viewers, this was a family of homegrown love and manners all melted into the wee ones' respect.

Now, dropping in at the grocery store to look for the very special hard candy made in Germany with its shapes of fruit in luscious color. The two precious bins were all gone. However, just one more look-see at the other products of temptation: cookies, breads and yummy more. There, hidden among boxes, were three glass jars of those coveted candies. I purchased two and left one for another's surprise. I will give one jar as a pre-Christmas gift. Then, tomorrow, I will go and find little individual glass containers, so I can fill four stocking stuffers. Kid's stuff!

While waiting in the checkout line, I saw the family of five shopping and the three youngsters helping to unload their cart. Dad guided their lifting to a safe space in the cart, and Mom tucked a hair lock away from the little Tom Sawyer eyes of one of her children. Another helped with light-weight boxes, and little sister looked like a Rebecca of Sunnybrook Farm. Such joys to see this family sharing in grocery shopping and never a complaint or whimper!

Twenty-Seven

Next, outside, I saw two children helping Mom to unpack the cart in the parking lot. I complimented her, saying, "You have such wonderful helpers!" She smiled and said, "Sometimes!" The keeper of the push cart was observing me with his great big smile, so I gave him a thumbs-up! Sister, in swift order, looked at me with a beautiful smile, and I waved to her with a big nod of approval. Manners are alive in households, and compliments of appreciation help to multiply these behaviors. Let loose and speak when you see these happenings!

Twenty-Eight

The day can't be completed without saying a thank you to my own family. The homemade chicken soup with noodles galore. The flavor laced with veggies, seasonings and lots of time in preparation. Two special take-home jugs. Leaving a very special necklace for repair so that the blue heart-shaped necklace can again travel around my neck. The other family discovered that the sewing machine stored in a playhouse now is no longer a relic and has come home. Yes, we all have those little stitches of memories and frozen soup for another dinner treat. Thanks, gang, for being my family. When this book title was introduced (*Just Call Me Mom*), a smile wound around the table as a signature of happily shared blessings.

Twenty-Nine

Where do silent thoughts originate in the busy minds of Moms? Do these have time and purpose enough to become new goals of achievement? Does this creative energy get lost in collecting the laundry and hitting the washing machine with all the needed detergents? This part of cleansing is a necessary element, but is there impetus for moving beyond the automatic actions? The autonomic nervous system has an inner reference in its race to catch up with creative thought. Stress builds up in this system, but doctors marvel at its speed and often lack the ability to slow it into safe energy. One doctor of noted acclaim from Canada to the shores of this eastern city said, "I just wish I knew how to slow the autonomic system down. There are no injections for this expressed concern, and I want to help my patients."

Some doctors care. That old country doctor always had office hours filled, but when there was a need, he made house calls with bedside manners too. A rich consolation in the voice of caring.

Like doctors, moms and dads are always on call, and it's hoped that the children recognize their twenty-four-hour commitment to lifting with helping hands. Manners exhibited in opening doors, pulling back chairs and seating with grace become habits absorbed rather than voiced. The teaching of awareness, sensitivity and thinking skills are so vital to strong foundations and success. Allow smiles, pats on the shoulder and a kiss on the cheek to express love beyond words. The unspoken is powerful and provides a satisfaction through seasons of change and growth.

But, sometimes, allow your voice a tone soothing to the mind, heart and ear: "I love you."

Thirty

Just Call Me Mom, and always living on the edge of the next unknown encounter. It can happen as fast as quickly crossing the street with no crosswalk. It can arrive when opening the door and out of the years stands a smiling face of so-long-ago, and a new adventure begins.

My encounter like this began with a first name and a sweeping hug, laughing, and a "Do you have time to talk?" We found a little round table with two chairs waiting and, during our intermission, little cups of ice water. There were cool moments of memories wrapped in batches, like reports cards waiting to be sent home. This beautiful colleague said, "May I tell you my story?" In my mesmerized state of listening, I attended a matinee that played out over two hours. There was mystery in old-time, war-torn love stories in letters fallen to her through inheritance. We passed intimate moments in cherish and trust discussing the stories. Afterwards, I encouraged her to write a novel. In reflecting on this now, I wonder, do I have a face that looks like a mom's to inspire such trust?

Next came an encounter that only the intuitive can explain. The electronic push pads on the library door opened quickly, and, making my way to the rest room, I found myself in front of a young woman who was singing spirituals of the heart. Her story quickly engulfed the mirror while my hands were soapy and wet. Her out-of-town-tourist trip had brought her back to the old south of her nineteenth century heritage. Yes, I was bestowed a rare treasure from generational voices of intermarriage. She confided in me that she felt different. I gave her a hug in leaving. Our paths may never cross again, but her shared story is already within the binding of the Library of Congress in my heart.

This mom is always on the lookout for the unique. On some days, stories seem to find this listening ear covered with short auburn hair. Never too frizzled or too sizzled.

Thirty-One

There's a peach-cream cloud riding the sunset horizon. Let your dreams for this day settle among the tree tops and come to rest near a fountain of praise, a day without the clutter of schedules. The coffee table is mirror-shiny clear, and the ice tea glasses on the table are waiting for a homeward-bound friend. There are fresh flowers in a crystal-pedestal vase to pay tribute to summer ebbing quickly away. There was no major effort. When it is done for a friend, the joy is waiting for another story. Musical notes and rhythms pour in through the open windows as the last warm breezes softly land on skin before time sends the gusts of chill. The ice cubes are melting, and the clock has ticked pass time for the doorbell to be pushed. You see, when friendship is strong, then it doesn't even require forgiving when the calculations have erred. Moms understand!

Time to put the steamer on to wilt fresh, leafy baby spinach and let the butter, salt and pepper be shared with a touch of apple cider vinegar. Food for the body, mind and spirit is ready to share now. The napkins hold butterflies winging like the day almost ready to close. The lawn cushions on the patio will come in just in case a sprinkle from the skies arrives, the last traces of a storm know as Maria. We've had quite a family of storms this season. The peach-cream cloud is smiling now, too. Thanks for sitting in on this little table talk.

Doorbell, and now we can catch up on lots of life not often reviewed. When good friends are coming, flexibility speaks respect, and no stress is displayed. Now lunch is quickly covered with cheese, crackers and then the planned ice tea and cinnamon crunch cupcake. Yes, we had calories to share as well as her surprise. It is not long until her birthday. Fun! Next time, it will be a pizza party for all of us.

Just being a mom in sharing that this young lady belongs on the joy-giver list.

Thirty-Two

To the Moms and the Mr. Moms, too: The 24/7 employment means that a high priority for taking care of yourselves is a must. If this neglected personal time is forfeited through giving to others, then you have less energy, and you need a heavy dose of "time out!" How? When? Where? The why has already gotten a suggestion! Here's just a little prescription for acquiring unlimited lift: At midnight, wake up for a drink of water, walk slowly, and feel your feet touching the floor. Awareness is your step in identifying conscious feelings. Whether through headphones or just ear listening, try music for the soul to rise into a rhythm of peace. With an inner thought of prayer so personal that no one knows you emit it across the night waves, send others your gifts. In this sending-out, you feel a rising above the humdrum, and you experience a newness that replaces the drained vitality.

Sit quietly in your presence, and when the cup of blessings begins to refill, a peace arrives to accompany the joy of who you are and where you are now. The rising dreams begin to excite you. When the cup of blessings overflows, then this relaxing time has been fulfilled.

Compose your own symphony of realization. Feel the grandest potential and purpose you have known. Take a deep breath and recognize the heavenly gift of just being you!

Thirty-Three

Good Morning! It's a cloudy day, but you can open the shutters on your thinking. In navigating the jungles of your experiences, set your own pace.

Sitting in a waiting room, a woman of great-great-grandmother status entered. There was no cane to assist her crippled and battered body. Slowly, she eased herself down into a leather waiting chair. At first, her face held a distorted, shriveled shape. Its size doesn't matter, but I observed the eyes of hidden color. Her hair was cropped short, and her arms twisted in a motion not of her own making. She might have been waiting for someone with a car to return her to unknown whereabouts. As she was seated, her legs bent into a distorted shape that may have been seeking relief. To visualize this picture of a dear, sweet little lady who held a bottle of Geritol, picture her elegance even if her bottle was empty. She was somebody special! We cannot fathom the configurations of life in her past, but in her determination, she revealed an endurance that we can't fathom. The moral to this story is that as we unlock our prejudices, there comes freedom through awareness of others and sympathy for their plights.

Do we ever take time to edit our thoughts and let the breath of life be renewed in deep appreciation? Create your own bright and shining luster for others to feel your warmth of understanding.

Thank you, "Man of the House," for granting sight to replace our continuing blindness. Are we judge, juror or victim?

A soft tear trickles down.

Thirty-Four

Oh, my! When filters are required, do we take time to see if there is a double thickness? Filtered thoughts just got mixed with the aroma of freshly cut grass.

Beneath the window, there's a university of young college men mowing the newly seeded lawn that was recently fertilized. If they belong to a fraternity, they won't require hazing to access this new position. Their dark hair uncapped, wearing safety goggles, they walk the mowers in an exercise regime marked by miles today. Just think that this may be the first job for each! How far up the ladder of learning will their footsteps take them towards the summit of corporate greatness?

Purpose takes strange detours during its execution. While making coffee and noticing the filtering sound, this little set of thoughts demanded to be shared. Exertion of effort can land soft on the keyboard being touched, but the energy released might be beyond measurement! At the close of each day, we feel a sense of accomplishment. Even now, this day is erasing clouds, and the sun is taking charge. Power up!

Thirty-Five

You never know when an ordinary day can turn into the most awesome one! In looking at my winging day, I feel wild anticipation of a guest at 2:00 p.m. to arrive. Our held-close sharing of life amuses us, and, in departing, we are favored by a pair of blue herons dropping in to visit the pond to fish. Of course, a camera caught action in reflections and a rainbow-in-arching in the sunlight. Just the right angle!

A short power nap, and the intuitive didn't check the clock which reported that it had become after 5:00 p.m. Oh my, not to smudge the day - a quick face touch, a chosen jacket of painted artistry, and out the door! The highway was rushing just like me, en route to accept an invitation to an Open House. Yes, the old-favorite-nearby library from teaching days has enjoyed a big face lift: no masking of high shelving, but openness now to all the hands that reach for beautiful books.

Wonderfully, the community held out welcoming arms to people of all ages, genders, races and choices as they wandered through aisles and table settings of grapes, cheeses, and cookies galore. There was even a small café with little tables, chairs and vending machines of drinks to soothe throats after all the chatting. Meeting rooms became welcoming nooks where, best of all, old friends hugged me and we put our lives back in touch. Life is bringing me the most wonderful 360-degree circle of friends, not lost or forgotten, but *found* despite the years of separation. In departing through the electronic doors, there was a cozy and warm feeling that this place will hold the old-fashioned community together. I've described not the old Norge Community Hall, but the fresh new life for the Norge Library. That's our old-fashioned hometown right here in James City County, Virginia.

This is where authors can enjoy giving their literary works homey shelves and finding security marked by joy and happiness. "Just call me mom" for finding again this place of welcome.

Thirty-Six

Good morning! Have you ever thought that the day welcomes you to whatever you have on your calendar, with to-do lists and dreams too?

This sweeping thought may drift from your desk onto the floor, or it may even jump with joy without being keyed into permanence. This thought with feeling requires space to explore your options. In reviewing the beautiful paper thoughts printed for consideration last evening, I saw that my "Open House" at a renovated library was filled with expressions of love. So, today I will consider options, some expressed and some hidden!

The little desk calendar has the word of reminder: "Open!" So, we'll allow the day to move intuitively and see where it takes us. First, open the windows with screens and allow autumn breezes to whoosh refreshingly into the living room of life. In bending the knees to give lift to the window sash, you might notice that a little hike around your outside world would be great nourishment.

Yesterday has given rise to enthusiasm for stoking energy a little higher. We have key hints of what might fill our day, and, if we allow, these may plant kernels to grow refreshing possibilities. Pages can be written, but it's you, the reader, who knows if any of these word-thoughts fit your psychological or philosophical needs. Ha! Already the spellcheck reminds of apostrophes or extra spaces required for thinking to be expressed clearly. Sit back for a moment, and rinse yourself in the day to find inspiration, enthusiasm and abundant strength.

Oh! The "Man of the House" just sent another refreshing breeze filled with harmony. Thanks for the company. See how reminders slip so gently into the day? I need to go buy the perfect "thank you" card.

Thirty-Seven

Welcome to a new day in which you haven't yet imprinted your majestic title of Ms., Mrs. or Mr. Mom! Those designations are a double portion of blessings. When your feet hit the deck running today, be prepared (as always) for unexpected surprises. Every day is a brand-new slate that you use to mark its lessons with scritches and scratches.

Now, please indulge me in moving from our fast-paced life to times past, where a little reminder is found on the backroads of a country setting. Just for a moment, hold the glimpse of a billowing-white-cloud bedsheet in the drying wind. It sails on a clothesline strung from a country home to a tall tree. This backtrack makes all of us appreciate the hot dryer buzzer when the clothes are warm and ready for folding. So, this is no drudgery compared to the time when the great-grandmas washed clothes by hand in a tub. We have those magnificent machines to do this work. Look at elderly hands and appreciate the evidence of great strength exerted so willingly.

When it's time to straighten the refrigerator, what a gift of preserving food for another day or two! In times past, the cold root cellar held the stock of food supply in sawdust if it were potatoes and canned goods on a shelf in a cool dry space. All the little things that are now commonplace were back-straining then. When you have the time to retrace a couple of generations that seem remote, realize how far these graduated improvements advanced. Now the old, relegated rocking chair from front porch days has disappeared, too, and no one sits there to lounge. There are still a few newspaper boxes sitting along the roadways of country living where the carrier drops off the news. But mostly today, the collection of news arrives on an electronic deadline. Just keep going into this comparison of our changing society. You discover yourself on an endless foray revealing how traditional thinking has bent around another curve to accept the creative and artistic dimensions.

This thinking evolved from my yesterday of floating on a ferry across a river, climbing a few hills and finding old-fashioned gingerbread in the homes of an historic town. I want to go back and retrace these elegant pursuits of the craftsmen. Only the camera can hold these treasures securely until the treasurable time of re-visit.

Now, have you investigated your own little attic thoughts? These weren't purchased from a big-box store; rather, from the very heart of our American Dream. We climb and sometimes slip back into the forgotten harbors of our lives. Grab hold and keep holding on to the joy of who we are now and the heritage that sustains us all. You have your own scrapbooks that can be tucked under an arm and shared at a family reunion. This last word, re-union, has new meaning.

Thirty-Eight

Take a recorder and cherish the voices of the past, if they are willing to recount the old-timey escapades of their childhood. There will be some tongue-in-cheek and rollicking-good laughing. If you happen upon a New England setting with the old pot-bellied stove and cigar-smoking-gentlemen sitting in heavy woolen shirts with feet propped up on a barrel, you will see that they are having a barrel of fun.

Move by the yardage draped along the side of the wall, and with your eyes, touch the thread, thimble and needle. Don't cut out these little savory moments; rather, salvage them just a little longer. The scissors have been omitted because you never know how much you want in the long haul.

Please, if you find a pickle barrel of old-fashioned salt and brine holding kosher pickles, try one. Remember, it's the salt of the earth that has been included. Yes, it is a taste of history that refreshes another new age. History is ageless, but sometimes it is told by dried parchment long ago stuffed into earthen jars and discovered centuries later along the Dead Sea.

I send you a big welcome to your contributions! I'm so grateful that we have met in heart, mind and spirit.

Thirty-Nine

As we surf again along the shoreline of our many hopes, dreams and accomplishments, let's seek some advice. We'll think of ourselves as a container having a great ride on the ship called life. In the shipping lanes, we stop for supplies amid adventures, travel and joy. There's another harbor that we need to enter, and it a big and busy place. So, a Harbor Master is assigned to keep these lanes moving smoothly. On this assignment, we are going to meet a CPA, an accomplished certified public accountant. We are going to seek his advice on the shoals that we must circumvent safely. This guidance will be for the households that hold the financial strength to keep operating in the safe channel. So, we'll ask for Council to speak!

Forty

In these side-by-side pages of *Just Call Me Mom* comes a soft stanza of music that may not be heard in the outside world. It may come from the fantasy vein that stays melted away in the busy flow of life. As an author, I'm not even looking into your eyes or on this page that is creating a harmony of feelings. Autumn leaves like coverlets float to the ground, invoking a memory. The miracle of each snowflake being different arrives, reminding us that we are unique from each other. There are apple blossoms in the next cycle. The heart moves in a romantic drift in its seeking to say who you really are! In the olden days, moms just never told their daughters about this mystical part of life. It's not a fall into a trance; rather, it is a gentler side of inward elegance that is discovered when you meet your chosen one. Already you might have experienced this, but to reenter this hidden world, allow your heart, mind and spirit to slip into a new wardrobe. It might require a shopping of explorative itineraries, or it just may already be hidden in the hope chest you stored in a distant past.

There's no disclaimer to be printed. It's those waves of love that have found acceptance and belonging. Every little silence is understood. When God sends His kiss of heaven, you'll never ask for a recovery prescription.

That's love! Smile!

Forty-One

It's Sunday, and the morning star high above the treetops greeted this mom. But in this fast-paced, spinning world, dark clouds have suddenly engulfed this precious view. If you ever wonder what makes a mom happy, ask her. There's no wisdom machine that would replace her. You must ask the mom.

So, let's venture deeper into the life of this person who wore aprons but never tied anyone to the strings. Loving to sew is suddenly a whirlwind of memory that inspires doing it again. There are slacks to hem, but the spinning and walking world lost the required threads. Letting loose an ocean of thoughts is another time indulgence that Mom loves. This ocean of thoughts for a few moments floods the beach and beckons the sandy toes to dip in its surf. That's Mom!

Try another gadget, and you will have put mystery of its purpose under her very nose. Take phone pictures that can zoom into the heart throb of delight. She smiles and laughs at the memories. Yeah, that's Mom! Capture her sparkle and zest for life in your gentle taps on the keyboard, and then you have an email of council to be sent for thought and lift. You may never notice when Mom has a heart filled with peace, because her secret is knowing that family and friends are close-by and safe and secure.

Learning new simple skills like creation of file attachments that send thoughts saying, "Thank you!" When the hush of home meets the floor lamp and a good book in hand delights her eyes through the beholding of others' talents. These are joys that don't reflect in a mirror. In the room, music plays. Happiness is a precious feeling of spirit in tune with the beat of its harmony. Music created by masters can fill emptiness when you take a leap into their worlds and make them your own. Blessings come to aid parents. Recognize that life is filled with awesome experiences!

Now, just another little slant of what life is all about: It's filled with learning. Everything can be a learning experience, even the neatly midnight-typed term papers that go from rough copy through spell check and are left on the top of your dash. Wow, we haven't even opened the thoughts saved in a bank of dreams. That's for another time and place! Just label this forever disclosure as a labor of love.

Forty-Two

"Ouch!" How do we explain temptation without having experienced those clutching fingers of doubt? Dear "Master of the House", please help this stumbling Mom where the left corn on the little toe is throbbing. That's kinda' the way temptation has a way of catching hold of our feet and mind too.

The early, early morning with the Morning Star broke the darkness and found the path again to this keyboard. I wanted another dose of shut-eye time, and yet the prodding was to hold to the earlier plan to listen to another great television sermon. The temptation while waiting was to just put off the sermon and return to the thrown-back covers of bedtime. I forced myself to fight the urge to do down that hallway back to the bed by searching for the channel, finding the cereal bowl, and waiting to move ahead. Even the chill of the body taunted my desires. Temptation is subtle with both positive and negative forces entering all options. Learning to discern temptation's sometimes subtle calling marks a powerful growth toward positive living. "Temptation" is an unpleasant word that jumps out of the darkened dictionary and cries for recognition. The redeeming light of love shrivels this thorn. Don't allow temptation to fester; rather, recognize it as a growth stimulus for the healing balm and giving "The Man of the House" personal-touch permission.

Sunshine and the counting seconds bring new appreciation for the seed of growth and four new leaves on the avocado. What new feelings have we discovered? "The Man of the House" has provided us with brave new strength! Again, thanks for the early-morning company!

Forty-Three

Hi, let's luxuriate in the sun pouring in through the southern windows! Homebody has just stretched across the pallet of now, bringing wings and brush strokes from invisible waiting.

Find *your* favorite sitting spot and share its views with smiling joy as the birds fast-blip past your sight. The tree standing sentinel to the autumn afternoon keeps adding new color to the leaves still holding forth. Beyond the pond, the bank up the hill to the big forest overseeing all this splendor is still carpeted in sharp greenery.

The clouds punctuate the afternoon in ever changing shapes, and to capture all these shapes in camera lens would be an unreasonable goal. So, as homebodies, we'll watch for a little while and consider why we haven't done this recently? The trusty car has a full gas tank, but it can wait for another keying to request directions. The mailbox will be empty, too, as all the statements are paid and staying home isn't costing anything today. So, the homebody can begin to check the calendar of the monthly special occasions, and let's list this one first as a reminder to do it soon again!

The body can relax in the home of walls holding welcome and security. There's no curfew on our time to just "be." No one ever showed us this skill of simply watching the world in review, leaving it to its own temperature control. Take a little recess (that used to only last fifteen minutes) from walk, talk and run like mad. Instead, pick up the book left at the page held by the inset of the cover panel, and continue. The one here is a trip back into the culture of strain and stress of other lives far away. So, our blessings increase without ceasing today. Have we found the spice of life in these time-out moments?

Let's go fix old-fashioned potato soup. The Irish survived on potatoes centuries ago, and these moments nourish us too!

Forty-Four

Hi to all the trail blazers of the world fitting into the Mom niche! Today, I'm taking memory capsules to fit pieces of a puzzle together of life before my birth. Its personal, but when some great-great-grandparent carried a baby son sidesaddle from the heart of Virginia to the hill country of the north, there must have been an inbred survival-of-the-fittest. The strata weren't in the geology climb over the mountains by the likes of a Daniel Boone; rather, the guts and determination to live and be free powered her onward.

This inbred vigor and vitality is still alive if we become aware of the gift to strike out toward new horizons. In fact, this lifetime just isn't long enough to fulfill all our inner yearnings. When there is no generational extension into the next, then find the words to say, "Don't stop! Go as far as you can to the end of the road!"

I found the end of the road when the pavement stopped in Canada and the mountain rose high. Exploring this region alone on a hike created a need for tennis shoes and bug repellant. You say, "Alone!" Yes, the adventure seemed safe, even if the end of the road provided a path through the forest a little further into the unknown. The sense of smell led to new adventure when the strong odors of life brought my senses to a stop to look down at my feet. There were tracks of life to be put into a plaster mold for the classroom science ventures! Hurry back to the beloved Airstream, grab the little pail with the plaster ready for the experiment. The casting went quickly, but the odor lingered with the question: Was this a bear or Sasquatch? With maturity on the side now of luck, we'll leave this answer to the far northern woods of Canada.

So, with a shrug you are thinking," Do I really know this inner Mom?" I'll share this in the secrecy of diplomacy: It's wonderful to exude a little mystery and leave it for the time of asking.

Forty-Five

What have we missed in our fast-paced life that has spun like a merry-go-round? Do we live and experience events without feeling the closeness to those we love? It's like thinking without saying the little things that glue us all together.

Was there ever the kiss of good morning that would not have been a warmth nourishing the soul? The little common things that were never shown in walking hand in hand, taking an arm and being so proud to be a couple. The unexpressed has surfaced in a big surprise! Don't allow emptiness to fill you and find in the afterwards all the missing emotions that were never found to be expressed. We know how to edit keyboard thoughts, but do we edit the things that were never spelled out as what should have been? Generations have grown up and have lived their own plans, but was this with awareness that others need intimate companionship? Just being present in body does not mean being present in the heart of soul-sensing love.

There's no time now to correct the lost years that have rushed by. Requesting forgiveness from past omissions seems untimely now. Allowing the heart of the soul to speak is the beginning of living to the fullest. This is not depression to think these things; rather, it is recognition that omissions allow us to slide beyond reach.

So, let's live! Let's go star gazing and discover the abundance of heavenly dreams being lit each night! Let's catch the stardust to apply to our eyes closing for rest. Then, when peace slips into its waiting space, there will be contentment and rest. A goodnight sent in prayers to all we love, and each one will always be welcomed home. Sent to all from mom!

Forty-Six

"Welcome back!" is what the manuscript screen is proclaiming. It's just not the same day as others. At this moment, the day shares a muddle of thoughts, lists and feelings. I am an ordinary mom! Please join me to accompany this golden sunrise morning of early-week October. We have music in the background to drown out worries. Maybe the spinning around of the desk chair will make a smoother ride. Let's go slow.

The tempo is ushering encouragement to organize effort. I'm researching, but first I will report that coffee is extending longevity. We'll all need a smack of that thought! Now I'll go and give the innards of the microwave a damp swish, and it's ready for a reheat. The microwaves aren't great for the brain waves, so protect those precious circuits that each of us have in operation. The stove top has some cooking crumbs, and I'll wash the liners on those too.

Time out! Wait for me! On the way, I'll turn off the floor lamp and save on the electricity. We'll all be grateful for no brown-outs if we are careful. Oh! The auto-recovery system just sent a little blue line reminder. Thanks!

Bingo! The tomato soup splash has disappeared! Pick up the red-handled scissors and get going on the stove-fresh makeup for guest appearances at Friday's dinner. Okay, the first liner looked tacky, so it was dismissed as last on the aluminum roll. Go ahead and laugh, but we really must be our own self-motivators. Almost done with the stove top, and my yen to do a picture-proof job is nullified. I would rather go look at the gnarled hands of a precious senior citizen who has wrapped life around history touched by her arthritic fingers. Her picture is a digital success! Oh, that circle of light is a reminder to finish the stove top! Now you'll understand that my creative bursts need picture-perfect images. Last night, I captured a full moon rising above the treetops that was framed in my triad windows. I sent this look-see shot to my publisher titled, "A Great Night Light!"

Forty-Seven

What a lovely gift! The sun just spotted the stovetop, and it's glistening bright. To lift the drudgery of that job, I had chosen a beautiful autumn-leaves-kitchen towel to keep me flying along. In sorting now through the junk mail stuffed in the mailbox, a bill is saying, "Use only black or blue ink to make any changes in address or emails." That means hunt, because I like to buy rainbow pens. Maybe today should be labeled, "Hunt and Seek?" Look, the avocado has lifted a new leaf three inches taller. We must be doing something right!

Time for the red-handled scissors and two new spools of thread to fit through a needle eye and hem three slack cuffs. The wash-and-wear sure are greedy when the threads are fragile and the outer wear is fashionable. Funny, the word, "thread" hopped onto the screen as "threat." Well, we'll fix that and complete the job that was put off too long. This may take ten minutes. If you ever have trouble threading a needle, put it against a white piece of paper. I have lots of that commodity. Makes see-through acceptable.

I just noticed a couple of pieces needing repair or touch-up. Moms are the best multi-taskers to fulfill any job description. We'll be a little smug and say that the business world borrowed the key to success from the hometown Ladies Aid Department. I hope you are laughing, because my silly tummy is jiggling in personal glee. We have 34 minutes to get these jobs done, as the drier is kicking up a spin right now.

Before it's forgotten, yesterday I spent $14.95 for a soft-bound book. That wasn't on my financial budget, but it was advertised as having sold around the world over a million copies. Wouldn't that be nice for us too? So, I brought it home to my condo, opened it up and found that someone long ago took the word from condom. Hope you are laughing too. So that's my money's worth achieved.

Oh, back to the needle and thread job - I love to play with needling words! There's plenty of light here in my living room and many chores still to be completed. But, time out!

Forty-Eight

Sent a good laugh to the publisher and threw the dried towels on the bed. Back to finding what can make the day different. One thing just arrived in the email that we have our Homeless Dinner preparations for next week. I'll search for an autumn-leaf-spinning visualization for those who used to carry their belongings in a black bag. Now they have motel accommodations that are clean, dry and hospitable. Our church, along with many churches in our colonial town, prepares food and materials for those in need. So, today we'll add thankfulness to our list of recognitions.

Motivation needs to be put into motion. We're rolling again!

Try double patience along with double thread to repair a button hole. Done! I've never shared that I'm not crazy about mending, but having learned to create a tailor back-stitch means I mend those slack cuffs in record time. Just point the needle to the left; pull up; take a tiny pointed thread through the attaching fabric; pull through; come back down in the same back-stitch manner; and off you go! This mini-home economics lesson originated from the teacher in high school who insisted that our very first sewing project was to make a pair of slacks. How awful can that be when I was never allowed to wear slacks until I was sixteen and had my personal revolting moment?

Oh, mercy! Sitting here with the windows open in the sunlight this morning is the first time I don't miss being in my classroom teaching. Look what you all have done for me! However, I have teaching goals, but they just do not hold forth inside the four walls of a single classroom. This new freedom has long been realized, but today in the "now", it is more meaningful. I just love being in motion with *Just Call Me Mom*. But guess what? There are other side-by-side manuscripts also bursting from the heart.

Forty-Nine

Times change so fast. While putting this manuscript into the printer hopper, up popped an arching rainbow on my carpet. So, of course, I shared it with my family, and I'm offering it to you to always be ready for the unexpected. I just grab my camera and we're off on another rainbow-dream arching and pulsing through the home and heart. Plus, I just sent an invitation to my daughter that as soon as she can climb steps post-surgery, she should come and spend days resting, reading, watching her favorite television and sewing. The latter is a passion she loves most of all! Her husband can join us for dinner and then go off to his evening performances. Now you know that I've just released a concern and an offer to be on their support team. We'll leave these lines open!

That's right, I need to pierce a few more stitches into those slacks. I wonder if the surgeon will use staples for his mending on-stage performance tomorrow? I did send my daughter a funny story, so that the laughter arrives before all is sewn up precariously. She will remember her Mom sitting on the steps of the Airstream after a rock-and-roll around mountain roads. The refrigerator door had become unclasped, and the gallon of milk had taken an adventure down the aisle of kitchen through the bedroom and into the bathroom. There was no "Do Not Disturb" sign. It never hit the holding tank. But before the cleanup project like HASMAT, Mom sat outside on the steps and ate Hershey chocolate candy kisses. Better than crying!

"Chocolate milkshake, please!"

Fifty

Hi, it's me again! Two phone calls for a little tight prayer chain on the surgery trip tomorrow. Then the stimulating conversation with Ohio distance family by birth blood, and learning of their troubles, activities and life in general. The most impacting statement for all of us: She said, "I just don't have enough of me to go around anymore!"

If you ever felt your life wasn't exciting enough, just step outside your front door and discover an ongoing cinema drama. It's that trip to the post office that holds waiting and sometimes surprises. The occasion was to seek two perfect envelopes for mailing books and a box for a seven-set of owls as a Halloween kitchen hoot. A couple next to me were busy trying to tape their packages, and their robust aroma exuded a need for spring showers. Well, I hurried into a line. A man with a white shirt began talking. "Do you like it here?" "Oh, yes!" I answered, ignoring his charcoal presence. "Where are you from?" he persisted. Finally, at long last the best answer to astonish him was to say, "All 50 states!" That was better than the man on the elevator, a handsome dude, who had asked me the same question. "Oh, I was on the third floor!" was my answer. Sometimes Moms get caught off guard, but the fourth ring finger is my guardian!

Searching for the perfect birthday card for a Master Artist was a challenge, until one just flew into my vision. It was from space, and I could reintroduce him to my latest book, *Sport's Alien Fantasy*. Just a little sneaky too!

The new donut-and-coffee shop was next to the turn out of the parking lot, but I resisted. Can I have a couple of gold stars for that? On to the other post office: add a special note to the birthday card and a stamp, too. Then the joy of a late-blooming magnolia tree right in front of my car. So, these are hanging in upright furls on the digital camera. These were like the blessings of earth and sky, just for me. At last, the lemony fragrance to purge other warm day clothing.

Then, walking back near the fountain which my condo overlooks, I encountered a little lady just walking and tapping messages into her phone. "Hello, you must be finished for the day?" She stopped, and here was a new neighbor who so willingly volunteered, "I'm a nurse, and if you ever need me, call!" So, we exchanged numbers and emails too. It's these everyday mini-views and feelings that make a lifetime movie with Technicolor credits.

You know? That maple-sugar-glazed donut and some fresh coffee would have been perfect!

Intermission!

Fifty-One

Hi, Family of Readers! There's a full moon just after midnight, and this warm fuzzy feeling just must be shared after a day when I can honestly reply to the question, "Where are you from?" Just call me Mom from all fifty states, where indelible memories pounce into word pictures.

We'll skip across the country like freely racing thoughts, where cranberry bogs were in little fiords higher than the roadway on a full moon night, too. You could almost feel the water ready to enter the roadway in a great sweep to be lost in the night. We'll see the redwood forests where the moss-covered trail winds down to the ocean and the sea air delivers its fresh history in whispered, private stories. Then the redwood chip under the thumbnail at a remote laundry, and an old woodsman looks up from his murder mystery and pulls out his knife. Gone the chip and gone my nerves.

Hiking along a trail in the Sonoran Desert and hearing rattles like little drums to learn that is the rattlesnake signal. Strangeness, too, at the end of the road in Canada when tracks are discovered that perhaps match a bear of mythical Sasquatch size. Not to mention the highlands where there is no movement of people and the autos sit silently. Remember with me the blueberries for picking by the handful or oranges strewn under the trees like little toys ready to play. My heart skips a beat when the armadillo crosses the marshy path from the clothesline and backs under the house. The next morning, the alligator swims in the Officers Club swimming pool. The military guns focus on a highway where protection is required.

There are so many mental pictures! The mountains surveying the valleys hold whipped-cream snow on their tops from a winter storm that also buttered the wheat, corn and soy fields. We recall rocks for climbing and hunts for gems; the fear of high, curvy mountain roads in unfamiliar surroundings; and hot brakes smoking.

Smell the glory of spring blossoms filling the air like a just-opened-perfume bottle! Or the lilac fragrances filling the airplane as it begins to land in northern country. The memories of Mom just keep coming: Lifting a video camera and taking charge of a wedding held in a little New England church in the woods. That perfect painters' paradise. The old antique stores speaking of auctioneers selling history, but now impossible to take a card. The beauty of the sea coast that lingers, meanders and follows the shoreline.

Fifty-Two

Memories outpour: The peaks of Mount McKinley, Mount Shasta, Mount St. Helens and others are far more exciting and entrancing in person than the pictorial presentations in a travel book! The boy's date is the queen of a festival in the city on the edge of a desert where true parades featuring camels, horses and gowned riders entertain in the forever-sunshine state. Cross rivers and streams and catch a glimpse of a flat-tailed beaver, or push deep into the mountains and see a real cougar.

Whoa! Little country church steeples and fields where battles were fought, lost or won. Listening to the richness of voices with accents and songs of the North, South, East and West. A capital of grandeur! From all fifty states, my stickers form a badge worn with pride.

Highways, byways and more to read to find directions. Driving in mountainous fog down the Snake River Canyon through a night of fear. Mom in charge of two little girls praying not to go over a canyon wall.

Studying on a ferry again in a shroud of fog on the way to a campus lecture and exam. Searching for the fault lines that underscore the beautiful house by the sea with bird-of-paradise in planters that complete a romantic picture. The sound of fog horns on ships on the bay or airplanes returning from far night maneuvers. The earthquakes that sway the stationary ceiling lamps in a school where we learned to duck and cover in precision. The water jug swayed, and the water reached waving dimensions.

The storms that quickly brew in the afternoon force us to run to close the windows from attic to the basement. The stories about house hunting would fill another book.

"Where's your favorite place to live?" The answer is so certain: to be living right here, right now, where I've finally brought my roots home. All the formals, suits and wearables are still on hangers behind the closet walk-in door. However, I forgot to say that window shopping for these was done as I drove to the school where I taught. Then I would call and say, "Save that size in the window!" I was a mom doing the original multi-tasking.

"Where are you from?" That story line about the stickers from fifty States is so true!

Fifty-Three

Who would have thought that a day will later be called, "homegrown?" This may turn into a morning-rising skyline with mottled colors. The depth and height of the day form a box filled with blessings: The agony of waiting for a precious family member to emerge from surgery disappears in the face of success. The pink-and-rose shaded camellia reminds us of the joining of earth and heaven. Blessings have unfolded through the prayers of warrior friends whose love and concern in this circle of life and love bring about a brief revelation of eternity. That may be a long sentence, but it has been a long time, if ever, that Mom has sensed this completeness with the "Man of the House" who supervises our space and time. What power there is in asking others in the halls of hospitals to encourage the hands of surgeons! Now the word "hospitality" connotates a deeper, more sensitive meaning among family and friends.

"Homegrown" is where roots are encouraged to grow and belong.

Prayerfully, thank you, Man of the House, for hearing! Your ears are great sensors, and we are the receivers of destiny. Coming together among family and friends to petition you, we get much accomplished, and, in the process, we become a larger family which is "homegrown."

Fifty-Four

Okay, Moms, Dads and whoever else cares to read: This isn't an attack about not having gotten the flu shot yet; rather, it's a demand to express this thought. It wasn't planned this morning, but here it is right this minute. If you are feeling the age of time on a chronological scale, you had better take another look at yourself. You are as young as you think, and you get the feeling to rise above this mountain of thought work. My inspiration comes from a little Indian girl in my classroom once. She said, "I feel like I'm my own grandmother's mother in a rocking chair today!" This stopped my time short! I ran it through the mill of shock, for it rocked me from my mind to my toes. I only had asked the children in school to think about how each one felt today!

There's a grinding noise beyond my window as the workmen bring my day back into focus. Now, I can begin moving on my list of today, as if I have just put the second reel on the old-fashioned movie-reel machine. Let your face welcome a smile on that one! Bye!

Fifty-Five

Hi family! It's 1-2-3-4- a. m., and a half page has been lost. It was all typed and ready to print, and I woke up! That's right, being a Mom is a 24/7 life regardless of the stage, time and place. When our eyelids close it is still on our minds.

This is to announce that two very talented and creative moms have been invited to join our trek into sharing deeply our lives through a new avenue. We are dear friends through the years, and now we hope to collaborate on this book, *Just Call Me Mom,* to add a third dimension! So, while they are working separately on their chapters, the grand debut has already been dreamed and ready to open along the riverfront in a beautiful shop in North Carolina. The Grand Opening, and book signing won't be avoided this time! This excitement will start with forming a caravan of adventure, racing through the miles and smiles!

A public broadcasting program not so long ago left a word that has stuck between my teeth like something needing to be flossed. It was an enlightening moment featuring the word, "misfits." That means simply something that fits but is different. So, not to miss this colorful transmission of a program about some marine creatures, I passed a whole hour of fascination that made a lasting impression. Just maybe we are misfits when we jump from one career into another and join new schools of exploration, like the marine life that traverses the ocean. We become writers, and our wild thirst for excitement to be on new stages eventually transfers to living documents on land-held pages. Complexities may complicate our swimmingly joyful writing. But in this case, the three of us authors of *Just Call Me Mom* (and our publisher) will climb into our capsule of flying delight. If we four are misfits, then please join our society of authors in search of adventure readers! Our genre has no gender division, so welcome aboard! Someone said recently, "When you don't have words to write, then call!" It reminded me of a friend with a shared career. She will recognize her contribution being a thoughtful mom who told me her life movie-story across a table of trust. A special "thank you" to her!

Sixteen thousand one hundred and ninety words now. We are filling our tanks of thanks with high octane.

Fifty-Six

When the intuitive kicks into gear, always it carries the element of surprise and runs fast as a cheetah. There's an adage about someone who would give the shirt off his back for a friend. Well, how about this? My family member may come home today, and my promises to help jumped into the thought stream.

When they left for their cutting mission to the capital city, they left behind bed covers thrown back and not back in place. I remember the prettiest sheets I have are those with the red and yellow tulips in green leaf pursuit. Just take off my bed, wash, and prepare for her homecoming.

Then, while the cycle of wash is on the delicate button, I make a list called, "What will make her home more welcoming?" Oh good, pick up big golden autumn sunflowers, if these are still to be found hurrying through the electronic doors of the grocery store selling flowers.

My efforts mean putting family first and skipping my plan to listen to poet laureates this morning. That would have been once in a lifetime; however, families are the first prize. So, no contest. Their lovely home in the country is beckoning for me to have their bedroom and kitchen waiting with warm charm.

The alarm clock just stamped another punctuation into this day. The temptation to take a short-break snooze had won. But, it's early, and the day plan has its own timing. First comes writing how living takes place to make a voice of concern, gratefulness and hope easier to understand. The gentleness of sharing brings comfort of healing warmth. Moms need rest, and sheets of love have already been placed at the ready! We must keep house with our acceptance of this gift, when the intuitive gives advice. Thank you, "Master of the House," for the prayer warriors who wrapped this young woman, my daughter, in bundle of healing health.

Sunflowers and homemade apple sauce sound appealing. Add a few other little strokes of a helping hand. No gambling, we can put steak and eggs in the same skillet. Mini size, of course!

Fifty-Seven

The maxi-view came as the sun shone through a golden veil of mist in the afternoon. A touch of blessings filled this soul. I had also found a dove feather, which from Indian lore is a sign of good fortune. Yes, prayers answered! The surgical hands of skills and miracles have brought our family closer together. Now it is evening with the promise of rain showers tomorrow, and tonight the air brings that smell of impending freshness. Our senses become heightened in noticing the protective touches from the "Man of the House." Yes, this is faith talking!

It's later now as I write this. It is the same time this Sunday morning as yesterday when this mom woke from a dream. Now I am tightly clutching a pill between my fore-finger and thumb. Wait, there isn't anything between these pressed-so-tightly fingers! That was a dream that had spilled over, but why? Do nonfiction and fiction suddenly meet in the night of dream study? Recognizing that my old character, Sport, had been waiting for another person to join for this strange and now nonexistent medicine. Pondering what ignited this dream, encased in a few seconds of memory for retention. What were the happenings of yesterday that triggered this dream of today? Was it the email from "Prayers Answered" and their comment, "More than you know?" Sitting here in the nightlight of bewilderment where fear had left a residue. But why? Is this a connection that says that after *Just Call Me Mom,* it is time to release *The Homing Signal?* I don't know why, but I sense a connection between the two books.

What will my collaborating authors and the publisher think about this strange link from dream world entering the real world of Now? This is Mom typing with head bent and not looking at the screen. Fortunately, there are only a few words to be edited, and the back space seems so unneeded. All that's left this early morning of Sunday is wonder, question and a little shrug of the shoulders.

Yawn, and let these brushes of miniscule dream float away like the golden mist I saw when exiting the grocery store yesterday. There's that old hunger pang in the center of my stomach. What will fill that space too? No not wine or coffee, just a glass of water. A delicate touch on the keys, so as not to lose this strange linking of thoughts, and now a chill! Turn on the printer and capture this page for our book, *Just Call Me Mom.*

Fifty-Eight

Walking to the refrigerator and looking at the sherbet glass filled with banana pudding left by one of my collaborators, this thought rises. Put it in the freezer and preserve it, like freezing dreams in time. Will there be a thawing out needed like the one required for the stone ripples formed on a rock during the Ice Age back home in my childhood days? Childhood play and adult dreams: Are these to be melted into reality? I only ate a quarter cup of vanilla bean ice cream before going to bed! Ouch, another chill! Wait, get a grip on the spring water jug and squeeze the cap with a firmness like I had in that dream pill. Swallow! Grape jam on toast because, maybe, purple will calm the brain. Haha!

When years separate, an overheard conversation without identification of person, place or event characterizes another mom's warm words, "I just want to stay home and have babies." This couple of an interracial marriage had produced one beautiful and very bright child, the apple of their eyes. Another is a beautiful moment of, "I had four babies in four years." Now, my sharing is that I went to the hospital to deliver two babies, but it could have been eight. Those extra doctor referrals took place over ten months each. So, let's laugh and recall that we all have a history of life and birth pangs and our gifts are in the creation of miracles.

Fifty-Nine

Question: How can moms wash away a sea of guilty feelings without creating a storm in the household? It's a plague that can engulf everyone, and how do we arrest this culprit of guilt? In sitting here listening to music, the windows allowing the soft gentle breeze of wind, I realize in a moment that self-confidence is the stopper of guilt. This is a glimmer of extra sunlight to lighten my weary load.

Allow "The Man of the House" to take on this negative burden and fast-track it out of body, mind and spirit. Wait for correct thinking to take its place, and then enjoy this peaceful release and the pool of renewed strength. Perseverance is a good companion to us when weariness creeps in. We create for ourselves a mentality of slavery to guilt. We can't always reach the outside windows to wash, so, to ignore imagined soot is okay!

My windows are raised and have screens to filter out the investigating wasps' or bees' unkindly stings. We can enjoy this freedom of Autumn floating with the clouds. I won't feel guilty now of not sitting in my favorite church chair this morning, as the moments of a sanctuary and cathedral ceilings on television are holding forth genuine peace. It is a hope that whoever rings the doorbell will find this here, too.

Find your own little haven and wrap yourself in warmth of knowing you are doing a great job as being Mr., Mrs. or Grand-mom. Happy Mother's Day!

Sixty

Just Call Me Mom, and another side never exposed: the one that jumps out of bed and races for the soap and wonders if there's enough to take a quick scrub. Then, in hunting beneath the sink, I find a little scoundrel soap hiding, and, sure enough, the flying dove of cucumber shades come out of hiding. Into the shower. Got a busy day ahead, and the see-saw of the short washcloth doesn't really release the all-scrubbed feeling. Then, of course, there is never a long enough wash cloth to do the job or anyone to assist. Hurry! The beautiful seashore towel will fit the drying needs as the little sandpipers race through the sandy picture. They never peeped when the thought came: Will there ever be anyone to be the last one out of the shower to dry down? That's a rule to keep the mildew from entering this quiet and showery place. Dry now, grab the purple bathrobe, and race to the guest room to the pushed-back scales for weight to be noted in naked edges. Sure enough, the lost weight is still on the surprise mark, so lunch can be a consideration after a shampoo and set on this beautiful sunny day. The kids are all in their own professions, and it's just me! Turn up the music and keep the day rolling smoothly in a rhythm fresh with a tinge of Wind Song perfume to rest on those shoulders.

Sixty-One

Let's get down to the nitty gritty part of Mom's feelings. If you didn't know Moms can have those crummy moments, then it's time to grab the crumb catcher and take a swift swish into a little dust pan. However, it's not the crumbs left on the table cloth that can be shaken off. It's those that require looking at the carpet and saying, "What's the quickest method of being ready for a new day?"

Answer: A new hand brush that can make a job quick, easy and most refreshing! Give the rooms a breath of air freshener and open the windows on the wholeness of breezes. When time is in a pinch, this may just help!

There wasn't even a thimble full of crumbs that fell to the white carpet, but the amazement is that the purple bathrobe had left little purple fuzzies for a reminder.

But just in case a crumb escaped the brush off, take the wet washcloth from the shower and give it a little face lift. There arrives a rewarding peaceful moment of mission accomplished. Join me!

Sixty-Two

My new entry here comes from a little urge to find a reward for emptying the dishwasher. Rewards are the "in thing" at many stores, so here's a freebie that I enjoyed today. Catch up with finger nails and glamorize the ballerina-slippers with polish as a fresh trim. The time for drying permits indulging a straw in a glass of juice. It's not the last straw, and it sure has a nice smooth feeling.

Yes, Moms have feelings, and these are usually left in a hamper with a lid. Meeting an appointment can also hold another reward. Go early and grab a seat in the world where aisles are filled with new releases on publishing.

The audience roaming through the stacks have their own stories. One homo sapiens sported a baseball cap. His hair dragged on the collar as his head tipped toward the boots. It really didn't matter the gender. There is no need to get lost in that pondering. This is a break-through involving leaving cabin fever on the back-home brick steps. Even the heavy rain of yesterday provided a delight in its heavy-duty, fresh-squalling wind-car wash. It's not foul to hit a cabin fever out of bounds with a fresh latte stirring the taste buds and a seat on the world.

Waiting for the appointment with ears of conversations about husbands and mixers hitting the ice crushing switch. The teetering chair seems to be getting impatient, but that's okay. I'm taking my dose of healthy living in a place I enjoy. I sit below a library sign. For you, it reads, "Read on!"

Sixty-Three

Now, if you have entertained retiring from your first profession, look around for what will keep your entertainment quotient alive! It's not the retiring, per se, that's important; rather, look at the divisor on the use of your time afterward. Be certain there's a space of at least six feet of sofa and not the underground kind. Then you want pillows to lean on, some with space for "head-for-a-nap." Be sure to keep an afghan handy to pull in additional warmth. Supply the coffee table with a big welcoming pen and notebook and glasses if you need them. Don't forget the personal stuff like tissue. your cell phone, the television remote, a cup of refreshment and a bottle of spring water. A napkin will heighten the color zone, and so will fresh flowers that are blooming beneath the glass top.

The house is ready for company, and, in the interim, there are seven books glowing from past publishing of dear friends and self. These are visible through the glass top. They are comfortable friends. In the distance from my sofa, I see there are collections of history painted on plates in gold trim. These are little keepsakes to maintain the Mom Happiness Quotient high, alive and comforting.

Yes! Even the finger nail polish keeps the shining touch of time well spent. You see, preparing for any alone time is important so that dreams may blossom through the rhythm of relaxing. You deserve this!

Sixty-Four

Dear moms and those-to-be! Have you ever wrestled with making the bed? It's like doing a rock-and-roll dance with the fitted bottom sheet. Which way do the printed tulips want to be placed? Right-side-up or upside down? The game of getting it into the right position is like a round dance in a terrain of dips and slides. There doesn't seem to be any waltz of the sheets when the double sheets are fitting in place. But try putting a king size sheet on a double bed when all four corners are fitted, and none seem to want to be snug-as-a bug in a frame. This is when asking for help is an exercise in communication. It also will create a sunny disposition on the hardest energetic job that the bedroom will demand. Well, I hope that you have laughed your way through making the bed, turning off the night light and finding this chore completed. If there are single beds to make, those aren't a challenge. because these have a way of allowing the offspring to make their own.

This morning, the linen snow showers are completed, and the pillows are plump. It makes for a serene picture of contentment.

Sixty-Five

Hi! This isn't any publicity stunt - it's that area where we all face control strings. Some are loose, and some are taut. My first to notice is the apostrophe that spell check says must be acknowledged. Well, that's not an issue to hit the stress button.

Now let's get down to looking in the closet for a clean sweep of seasons' hanging stuff. Skip the uniform look of the jumpsuit that is such a comfy addiction. There's a new blouse with the tiered neckline, and it matches a pretty, purple set of slacks. Mercy, these match in color to almost a "tee." Then the scarf twisted into a butterfly infinity matches, too. Whee! Let's get our act together and dress for our own satisfaction. It's a good feeling to not be in that dumpty-couch-sitter position. Then, let's find a nice place to go visit, and maybe take the camera to capture a purple orchid too. You see, we so often jump to what other people dictate. That's a mark of control so elusive.

After the closet, there's the medicine drawer that isn't any pharmacy, but it has its control wording too. If your numbers don't meet the prescribed set of values, you lose a confidence level. This can cause an ulcer that someone thought might be deep within the innards. If someone says, "Open your mouth," then stop and ask why. You see, the voice of experience here got a photographic camera shoved down the throat with, "Swallow!" That maneuver took fifteen years to regain a singer's heart-soprano voice. No ulcer yet!

Now, go ahead and allow your mind controls to deliver your own piece of mind. Personally, I know that reviews are important to the success of any book, but more important is the author's own sensitivity that the writing is relevant. This just feels good!

Sixty-Six

Dear Readers: First, this isn't a how-to-do-it book; rather, it is one that just wants to be expressed. We'll label this little epistle, "Dress rehearsal," and it is especially for an empty-nester who must do the whole gambit alone. Here goes:

Getting the box of bills and accumulations out just seemed to fit on top of the freshly made bed. There was little comfort in that calculator-diminishing account. In amusement, to prolong the ordeal, I decided to sort and then take a power nap. That would help, but on the humor side of it all was this thought, "If someone comes to call and inspect the house and fix the ceiling, a quick throw of a quilt over the top would cover up the job." Sure enough, the sun came out and the phone rang before the nap could receive any encouragement. The Parish Nurse will come to visit! I rearranged priorities to get out the purple outfit, scarf and all, and wear it for company coming. So, dress rehearsal became a must-show, and she would have to accept either tea or coffee, regular as my choice.

Now, time for a nap, as this article insisted to be immortalized instead of being rolled into oblivion.

Sixty-Seven

Dear moms, when the crescent of morning begins to filter into the day, here's a little thought. Look out the window, discover the panoramic sunrise and note that this can also be caught later in the kitchen skillet. When boredom catches a thread of discontent with the usual breakfast fare, here comes a colorful item.

Heat the skillet slowly while a thin bagel is popped in the toaster. No, we aren't doing the jelly routine. From the refrigerator, take out a box of liquid egg mixture and pour in just a slight yellow circlet of egg. Throw in a thin slice of honey ham and a sharp cheddar cheese slice. Out pops the bagel, on goes a tinge of butter and a thinly sliced onion and chive cream cheese. With a pancake turner, merge these delightful ingredients into an elegant sandwich. Cut it in half if you have small eaters. This will do for two. If only one, share it together, or put it in a freezer bag and finish it off after an unplanned dash to the post office. That's you!

Sixty-Eight

At a meeting once, a remark was made, "Some never know when to stop writing or painting their project." Well, just wait to hear this new escapade that is as fresh as the footprints left behind.

Waiting through several seasons of needed repair, the temperature control in the condo was finally determined for a replacement that would provide mom with a new lease on life. That's not the temperate kind; rather, it's one that fits the changing season of air condition and heating. The unit had left some inner temper tantrums that were not addressed until this day and time. The intuitive took a vacation while the three gentlemen arrived, all equipped for their repairs and installation. Up the step ladder atop generous sheeting to protect the carpet through the hall, one promises, "You'll never know we were here when we are finished!" I had the thought, "These gentlemen have been well trained by either moms or their employer."

Then their employer came to tell me, "We put a foot through the bedroom ceiling!" All I could think was, "I wonder which painting took a hit?"

It turned out that the little extra bedroom with the shredder, notebooks awaiting editing and Christmas decorations that had never made it out of boxes was the room that had taken a visitor of surprising size through the ceiling. I'm sure the eyes of Dr. Albert

Schweitzer, framed in portrait, had viewed this intrusion as off the wall.

The yellow insulation above the ceiling also had danced through the hole from the attic and had found home on my floor. I haven't gone to inspect the ceiling invasion, as it will be repaired. Fortunately, no one broke a leg in this stage performance, and we can move ahead with an encore of applause. The new unit is now a welcomed resident in the attic.

Signing off now from *Just Call Me Mom*!

By the way, I love to be called, "Sport." It reminds me of my alien fantasy.

THE PURPLE BATHROBE

One

This novelette was first begun in a notebook called, "BE HAPPY!" That's right, this purple garment has a way of making everything cozy, warm and interesting. So, jumping ahead, let's discuss the fact that this morning, after cancelling a lovely birthday dessert invitation due to weather of blustery beginnings, the purple bathrobe accompanied me and the long black-and-white dressing gown back to snuggle in for another snooze. That's not the kicker. Here it comes: From sound sleep, the wearer of the robe was woken by her name being shouted! No, the phone hadn't rung, the doorbell hadn't sounded, and it's a rarity for her given name to be spoken. Wide awake, and the Purple Robe has been known to listen and speak on occasions, so get ready for little unexpected moments.

"Did you see the college kid walking down the street wearing a caution-yellow jacket?"

"No that has nothing to do with my being shocked out of a sound sleep!"

"Oh yes it does!"

"Caution! You are edging between dreaming and the mysterious! Don't worry, today my computer and printer aren't speaking to each other, so this is not yet in print! Even the cursor is being contrary, and it jumped back up to the shout! I think it's time to go build a pot of beef stew."

While chopping the veggies, out popped, "Now, you be careful of that dull knife you are using. You don't have band aids and no one to fix a bloody finger, let alone drive you to the ER."

"Yes, and you certainly do look out for my bod. Well you certainly disclosed my singular status. Shhh!" Without cutting too deeply into the culinary skills, I proceeded to wash the big bladed knife with a new soap scratcher.

"You have never put a soap scratcher on my back!"

Two

"I do have to be wary of you and your kitchen skills. You just left a hard-boiled eggshell get splattered all over my dressed-up look."

"Sorry, I didn't know you were so sensitive, but, after all, you have to be a little more mellow in your age stage."

"There you go being sloppy - an egg shell just hopped over onto the keyboard, and we will need a needle to prick it off."

"Thanks for the hint."

"You can certainly get yourself into little needling jams!" Aren't you glad you have me to keep you in a good mood?"

"Right you are, and don't remind me that I sneezed. We saw this morning that there are thirty-eight million people in the country who have or are into the flu miseries. I caught it with my bent elbow like we've all been cautioned. The other act of excellent hygiene is that when the kids go on their cruises, they rub elbows with greeters rather than handshakes. Cruise? What about us? I only have one passport and won't be allowed to take an oversized robe in my luggage."

"Ouch, you just hurt my feelings! You may be sorry when the overly long gown makes the trip. Why is the loaf of bread wearing bent slices?"

"That's because it got squeezed too tightly in the basket."

"You mean like you squeeze me to get my belt in place? Just look how you have left me looking crummy after enjoying your toasted egg salad sandwich and tomato soup."

"You don't need to complain. You are going straight into the washing machine on the gentle cycle."

"Will the drier be on the gentle cycle too?"

"Definitely! Then I'll put you on a hanger and let you cool off."

Three

"Hey Sport, you are getting forgetful. You left your Christmas tree nightlight on in the hallway all day!"

"Oh no, that's not the case at all. You see, Christmas can be every day! That is my case when getting up every morning and thanking the Lord for another day of beauty and wonder."

"Thanks for sharing your inside-out feelings!"

It's time now to begin at the beginning and write as it has happened. The Saturday after the New Year's Day has sparkled with snow deep and ice sickles lengthening. The purple bathrobe breaks through in culture to join in speaking. The ties are tight, and the strings inside are secure too. Laugh your way into what this magic piece of robing may bring!

"Purple bathrobe, I surprised you that Monday morning which was being observed as the holiday. You got tucked into the washing machine with three lady gowns. A little heavy as polyester is just two fewer slots. You'll manage just fine, but the drying cycle required an extra touch-up of heat to dry out all those wrinkles. I just heard a big sigh from you that this escape is over."

"Gee thanks Sport! I'll get even with you while cooling off on that big hangar!"

"Now calm down - there aren't any dare threats at this house! I just enjoyed a new set of ballerina slippers. Now, to put on shoes for a day of lists left on the desk. It's an umbrella day, but I'd rather write, type and go for some excitement. A jumpsuit is a good starter. Funny, but a play invitation was asking for male actors to try out for auditions. The title is called, 'Rip Cord!' We'll have to wait and see if the two who were sent this invitation decided to jump up on the stage and perform for us. Dear Purple Bathrobe, if so, I'll sneak you into a knapsack for a surprise disclosure. Did you catch the camouflage word of clothes? A real show-stopper! Sport always stands and claps at the end of encores! I just might shop for a bright purple necktie! No, not for you to wear! It's for the other silent purple bathrobe. Shhh!"

One gown returned wrong-side out!

Four

Back to the beginning, on the Saturday after the New Year - Laugh your way through what this magic piece of purple robing may disclose.

In the middle of the night, a need. Wake up for a cup of hot coffee. You can have hot chocolate if you prefer. Now I remember that I am staying in a strange house of family-keeping-warmth because the heating unit at my condo said, "Time is up!" Well, while pouring water in the cup for microwave, a blooper happened. The small cap jumped into the cup when the jug said, "Ker-plunk." Wrong cap and wrong size. The old standby robe said, "So what? Your purple fabric has a way of comforting skin, mind and soul when the heart is ready to burst beyond confines."

Shhh! This novelette may become a long story, but, no matter long or short, it is just seeking to find the other purple bathrobe. Go ahead, laugh, but it is safe to say that sizes seem to fit all these days. I prefer a size with room to spare and pockets deep for secrets kept.

Oops! A sneeze jumped right into the elbow, and the sleeve said, "The Wind Song perfume is spreading out across the fabric like a spring breeze. You never know - it might intoxicate the nightcap."

There's a new wine waiting on the top shelf at home, and it comes from a mysterious land where grape wine dances in delight. Unopened, and the name will become like the bathrobe: a symbol of lingering smiles. The heart is daring, but the pen isn't very brave this minute. Dare I to say, falling in love is like growing roots on a new grape vine? As it climbs to the surface, it reaches higher for tendrils of strength. You didn't know the purple bathrobe is rooted in life's little sharing moments. Pull up the afghan, close the eyes and allow dreams to build. What will tie to the robe and cover it with a shield of peace and happiness? Searching, yes.

Five

Can dreams reach out beyond chiffon curtains and find sunlight? There is an oasis somewhere - let's go find it! When crossing an ocean where angel fish swim amid coral reefs that hold mystery, the pillow case begins its heady journey! Dreams are like that! They get interrupted.

Another day of fresh new thoughts and purple comfort in the culture of high demands! I can stand light and glare! Here's a peace for dreams and times beyond now to ease into reality. Take a drink of spring water to quench the throat after a long dry spell of missing family birthdays and holidays. All it took was the besieging of a flu-double-dose-needle-prick to sign the fate of lost joy! It was ordered and later given after the health had been proclaimed by two doctors, "You are in great shape!" Well, the shape is hidden now inside the purple robe which has ten pounds less to cover. I'll just zip up the slack suit and my lips too. And try to regain strength to wait to live again. I had a close call, twice.

Smile, even the lint gracing the carpet is silent. "La Canada" is swaying across the air waves, and it fits the winter of rescue. My family brought the four-wheel drive with the horsepower to fly above the icy snow spikes in the streets to save me.

As you have guessed, this is just a hometown pen leaving itself open to fresh thoughts. I am sitting here at their dining room table and allowing my thoughts to drift out onto the deck, where a squirrel is attempting a ballet routine in the snow. The tall, beautiful bamboo trees stretch toward the blue sky. This natural forest is shared with pine trees, too, and it hovers over a waiting deck for spring plantings. There has passed a winter of waiting!

Past living in warmer climates leaves me with lingering questions of "what if?" We'll let these meandering waves of the past just drift away! Maybe this quiet hideaway is a retreat for healing. Time stands still for this author when writing takes the helm of this little ship.

Right now, it feels like my ship is on a shoal and unable to move. Maybe there are questions requiring anchoring, and these hold tightly inside the purple robe in a place that no one can suspect. There is a hidden love caught in the windless inner self.

Six

Now a spray of "Shout!" to clean away a coffee smear, and this, for me, is a simple hint to rub the past away. No, some of it is beautiful, and it would never be forgotten. This isn't any depression like a canyon that some have traveled on slow-donkey plodding. This is just a recognition of the rim and sights along the way toward a new summit!

Germinating thoughts agitate me on my fresh white pillow case. The warmth of this moment nudges the pen to share that the purple bathrobe might have learned of another purple robe, too.

Does one dare to venture into dreamland and allow unfolding stories to become a fabric that is measured in lengths of relationships? I dream about a novel that will sweep right off the bathroom shelf and become a living resident of my home.

Smile again at these warming trends toward a fashionable, romantic stroll, as winter's closure gets sealed in the springtime of love. Strolling without touching, dreaming without slippers - just a touch of heaven. I am hopelessly happy.

Can a little book such as this nourish us so that we live as a new generation of warmth and surging emotions? This is a tiny book of creeping emotion towards borders where no passport is required to the land of human love. Two people who have never held hands just became spiritual lovers without lips ever touching. Only from far distances. What ignites this spark of love in this New Year?

How can a wild dream created in the sleep of seconds' duration emerge awake and filled with so many plans? I must jump up and nourish these with hot chocolate and cinnamon toast. Today, my memory is holding close to me this dream adventure without the exertion of energy on my part. Unlocking the dream world differs for everyone, but the secret combination to this author's safe of dreams is delicate. As for you, tighten your grip on the free revelations of subconscious passions that arrive on the murky paths of your dreams!

Seven

"If you think hanging on the bathroom hook is entertainment, you are all wrong. I missed out when you took my telepathic advice and hung up the matching blouse and slack set of yesterday. Okay, I was a little miffed or jealous that you so enjoyed that perfect match! The phone rang, and we got interrupted, but that's okay too. It was the repair man wanting to replace the big-foot hole in the ceiling."

"Purple Bathrobe, you would sure have felt good on top of my already-dressed condition. The repairman got lost and couldn't find us. In the neighborhood, the pond is a good landmark, but he still was lost. In going out in the sunny winter temperatures, it felt like spring was too far away. He got here, finally, and, to my amazement, he pointed out the long foot mark that marked the wall after the accident in my condo. Whee, a close call for that young Marine! No broken limbs, just a broken ceiling during the positioning of the two-hundred-pound heating unit in the attic by several men. Thank you, Lord, for your care during that nail-biting moment! You know, I think I'll put on another polish of the nails and put the next repair installment on the calendar! I don't run a drop-in like a convenience store!"

Eight

"What brought on the spray bottle to clean the mirrors throughout the house?"

"Now, Purple Bathrobe, you really are keeping a close tab on me. I'm a very private person and don't have to account for my unexpected actions."

"Oh!"

"Well, the nail polish triggered the polish thought. Multitasking is a need for this lady of the house, and that is what brought on that extra event. Hmmm, I always must chase around the screen to find you, dear little pink pill. Why do you jump all around and I have to play hide and seek with you?"

"Well it's similar to your jumping from one escapade to another, just like giving the carpet another brushing."

"Oh, I didn't want to say anything and hurt your feelings, but there are little purple threads and fuzzies that cling to the sofa, afghan and carpet. Getting ready for tea somewhere between two and four o'clock reminds me of my school days."

"What do you mean? I never got to go to school with you!"

"Well, when we had truant children or sick ones for a long period of time, the school nurse was sent out to check on them. Now I have the parish nurse coming out to visit, and I've been truant from a church pew for a few months. I don't have to live in a bubble to remain healthy, but it appears that this winter, that was the action plan. Then, too, when I was doing graduate work, I accumulated enough credits to have a Social Workers degree. I only lacked 100 hours in a clinical setting. So, I'm sensitive to the process and will just enjoy pouring a cup of orange/spice tea and serving little cinnamon tea cakes. I even lit the tiny old-fashioned candles to relax the table scene. I hope this has quenched your curiosity, dear purple bathrobe friend."

Nine

"Why are you bubbling in giggles when I don't understand why you made me lie on the floor with my arm up waving? Then you had another shot at my neckline resting on a hibiscus pillow with purple and yellow blossoming, too? Just what are you up to on this new monthly set of dreams?"

"Shhh, I'm sending one of these photos I just took to our publisher and with the surprise that we have invented a talking purple bathrobe. I think it would be hilarious if it turned out to be a book of years, and what great success if, in the reading, one discovers that daisies can talk, too. So, your arm up means, 'Hello!'"

Ten

I just got back from running errands and find that a runner has taken a hint from the reinforced toe. It's easing its way toward my ankle right this minute. Someone will say, "Why do you wear hose? Just go barefooted!" But that brings up a red flag of a childhood display of bare feet. Bare feet seemed to be so intimate. Once, an unexpected young church member came by to say, "Do you want a ride to church this evening?" and he looked at the bare feet. I had that horrible feeling of being naked right at the front doorstep. Let's skip past the errands. I'll share that the Purple Bathrobe now comes to life in a new purple notebook, which meets eyes of approval. Shopping has its sealed-in feeling of success when the only expenditures created are minor ones. It's like going to the candy counter and looking longingly at the white chocolate or caramel fudge. That was a long time ago. Now it's the printer paper package and a new notebook for hard-copy proofing that creates an air of freedom to indulge. I'll slip the three-hole-punched-notebook papers in quietly while I remember a two-year old shooting questions to his pretty Mom. I loved to watch the two communicating. She tilted her head back and showed his cute little face language that said, "I'm not listening!" Kinesics is such a fascinating communication tool. He ran down the aisle and picked out two long sticks and pretended to play them like drums. The pretty Mom with cool quiet never said a word. She just tilted her head up again. I'm so happy that in my aisle running, I met those two to introduce Purple Bathrobe to a new word: "kinesics."

"Why must you always be teaching me to learn more about how I should behave? Today is so pretty, and just waving, 'Hello!' was such fun."

"Now you have the right idea, because we do have fun sharing where nothing is off limits. If couples would just learn this in the high school marriage and family classes! I know the instructor would shudder even in the twenty-first century to allow the word 'bathrobe' to enter the curriculum. There I said it!"

"Gee, you make me feel so wanted and appreciated!"

Eleven

"Mercy, in oversleeping, all kinds of things keep creeping into the day. Walking into the living room, I notice through the windows that the day has its own moody and cloudy personality. There's a huge dark cloud that extends in all directions, and we're going to have to watch what it is going to shout!"

"But you never shout!"

"Thanks, Purple, for noticing this. I really search for the harmony that we are all capable of feeling. So, let's hit the restart engine and get a jump on today. The key is to go back and catch another glimpse of what our bathroom is telling us. Many little ads have been cleverly placed for our morning viewing or goodnight blessings.

"I just noticed the first welcoming note, 'The New Look!' Don't consider this a brush-off of snarls in the hairdo. That is fixed with tomorrow's quick shampoo and set. But it looks like our intimate time of fun in the bathroom must be delayed, because the hole in the hallway ceiling is about to get another shock treatment. Buzz, cut, measure and make it look like new. Outside, the horizon is drawing a dark curtain, and one white snowflake just whizzed past.

Even the bark on the little birch tree is shivering. This may just be quite an interesting day. The washing machine is croaking a spring-time serenade that can be heard by the creatures freezing by the pond. Painting this picture of outside will have to wait until a new canvas can be purchased and joyful paint kits are reviewed.

"Come on, Purple, don't hang around pouting because the green-zippered robe was my grab-and-run choice this morning. In fact, I saw several cozy robes in magazines in the middle of the night and will have to consider the sale pricing as being right on track."

"You mean that my thirty-year friendship is going to be put out to pasture like the old horses?"

"No, dear Purple Bathrobe, you aren't an antique! You are my closest, funniest wardrobe pal. You seem to hold the key to my life and all the hidden stories that want to sprinkle out of me like salt and pepper. Oh, have you heard a new word discovery, well, it is one to me? It's called the generation of 'preppers.'"

Doorbell!

Twelve

"That seems to fit in to prepare for another busy day. Those 'preppers' are those who hang their hats on worrying about the end of a book. Enough said!"

"Thanks for teaching me vocabulary that seems to edge right into a new dictionary. Do you have a bathrobe course to teach?"

"No, dear Purple, this may never even hit the conveyor belt if our conversations fall off the screen like a bowling-ball-novice plunge."

"What is a novice?"

"Well, in keyboard-layman terms, its one just learning to add a bright spot on even one person's day."

"Why did you add bright?"

"That's because the sun just summoned a little crack in the sky and allowed a smile to come for a visit. Dear Purple, you keep me feeling alive, warm and loved. Wrap yourself around my office chair, and we'll keep our friendship strong and comforting. That's what friendship is all about. It's companionship that leaves breathing room to never suffocate but, instead, to hold tightly profound love with understanding. Did you ever hear of silence holding people close without proximity holding hope? (Oh! An extra 'o' hopped in like a little balloon that can add color.)

"The ceiling wallboard is see-sawing back and forth, and we don't need dust to add to this morning. I'm really getting brave, so I went in and closed the door to avoid the dust particles that claim lungs. Everyday living seems to creep in and settle, and I hope it can reveal that our own fast-moving life really doesn't have to be a merry-go-round in the status quo, but it can launch us into the extraordinary. Boy, Purple, can't you just visualize if we were ever invited to make a speech? I'd drape you over my shoulder and wear my purple blouse and skirt to match. The audience would get the idea that we aren't a mix-and-match, but great buddies."

"Would you give me a camellia corsage to wear like those prom wishes?"

"Oh, my goodness, I just remembered that I have an author friend who makes masks. Do you suppose she could make you one to wear on special occasions?"

When word freedom can be given full reign, look what can birth new ideas! Dear reader, stop critiquing your own creativity and let the world meet you, too! Life is a great big puzzle, and it's so much fun to put together the pieces. Let's go exploring! Maybe, our efforts will provide someone with a key to their own greatness!

Thirteen

"Sport, I just saw you go and start to fix the coffee pot for a fresh start after the shopping expedition, so isn't that being a 'prepper' too?"

"Okay, Purple you may be right, but our reasons are different. I like to come in from a cold, 43-degree shopping spree and hit the start button on a fresh after-four-o'clock cup of warmth. When I get back, I'll tell you about another 'prepper' situation that is exciting for the next march toward springtime."

"Must I wait?"

Fourteen

"Sport, I'm so glad that you woke up realizing that I've been watching you struggle to get your arm out from under the covers. You were twisting my arm to get the release of the sheet, blanket and quilt from holding a tight grip."

"This is curious because, apparently, dreaming moves us from the depths of sleep into the external world of show. I remember waking, and there was my outstretched arm with my hand ready to receive a piece of paper. It felt so strange to see this extension of my left arm motionless and my hand empty. Of course, being awake means questioning the value of getting out of bed and trudging to the keyboard. This yen to record the nonsense resulted in being caught in footsteps through the living room filled with moonlight strong and beautiful. The wet tears forming were evidence, too, that something important was being given to me."

"Well, I'm glad that you let me rub your face and dry your tears."

"Sure, Purple we do share a lot, even the crummy times that leaves a little chill at 1:30 a.m. In fact, that creates another urge to fix a piece of toast. However, the image of my outstretched arm and open fingers still leaves a strong image of mystery. Right now, I'm going to press the printer into action and release this page from its holding. I will re-read it in the morning, wondering again what was so important on that paper? Was it a document to sign or one to smile and have placed in a picture frame? Dear Purple, thanks for keeping me company."

Fifteen

"Hi, there, it's ME!"

"Sport, why are you scurrying around like a little squirrel this morning? I saw you giving the coffee table a fresh shine and hand brushing carpet fuzzies and crumbs. Plus, you swept the kitchen once more."

"Now, Purple I don't tell you everything, and since we don't have an old party line like the '6042-blue' back in the kid days, you can't listen in. Also, I don't share my emails except in little stacks hidden in notebooks or a drawer."

"I know, I can see, and I sure feel left out!"

"I'm so sorry, but there's a dividing line between private and professional life. You are my very private life, and today our professional life will be discussed, but I need you to understand being tucked in the bedroom. Our publisher is coming to plan for the next step in which book to publish. You and I aren't ready to share our 'Purple Bathrobe,' so when we are ready, you sure can speak up and tell him your thoughts too. He will probably laugh, and that's a very good sign that your own personal and professional life might merge."

"Okay, I'll be patient a little longer, but it sure is hard waiting to have my debut."

"And I'll never tell your age, because you just never show your wear. Now, I've got to rush and get ready for an exciting afternoon. I've got tomato juice doctored with some spices, chips, fresh avocado dip and baked scallops wrapped in bacon."

"You have never used 'wrapped,' except around me. What temperature are you heating up?"

Oh, much too hot for you at 450 degrees!"

"Ouch! Okay, I'll hang around and wait!"

"I'll throw you a kiss as I close the door, so your listening ears won't ring."

Sixteen

"You just don't understand that I have feelings and this one is from abuse!"

"I don't understand what you are talking about."

"Well, while you were mixing the tomato juice and Worcester sauce and mixed-in salt, you dropped a little on the counter. That splash hurt my feelings as you wiped it up with your forefinger and on my pocket. Now, I don't hold grudges, but can't you be tidier? Hey! I just got a whiff of lavender-and-vanilla spray here in the hallway and bathroom. Smells good, but I also noticed that you are wearing a skirt, and as someone at the hotel said a while back, 'Well I see you have legs!'"

"Oh, for goodness sake, I love wearing skirts and dresses, but there is such a limited supply of these in my collection. Dear Purple, you sure know how to get under my skin at times. We'll discuss our wardrobes another day. I'm so excited, and three o'clock seems to dance so slowly with the minutes and seconds. Time for ballerina nail polish and plenty of time to dry."

Seventeen

"Sport, you are so quiet today and I know something is touching your feelings of need. Will you share these moments with me now?"

Dear Purple, I learned yesterday the motivation for readers searching for their perfect book of escape. They want intrigue written for the erotic mental stimulation of their personal and secret passions. I'm at a loss for how to find words of expression in my quiet hours of writing and thinking. What book will open from keyboard to the hardcopy notebook? Little chips of wisdom to reach readers may have to be given over to another's gifted wisdom. These word-thoughts have triggered a powerful sneeze."

"Then don't look so glum, lean back on this chairside moment and enjoy the mystery of yesterday. You didn't tell me not to listen to the distant hallway conversation of the discovery found in your Bible in Revelations. You had carefully found a little wooden picture frame and placed it inside as a saving reminder that someone out there cared. I heard you catch your breath the first time you read this magnificently worded thoughts of inner love that had no signature. It had no addressee and no signer of who might the writer be."

"Yes, Purple, it took a lot of courage to produce this framed piece of loving thoughts and ask, 'Did you write this?' The other purple bathrobe owner leaned forward, carefully reading, examining what might have been an old yellow piece of paper. He said, 'No, you have someone who feels this way about you?'"

"I'll bet you were even more shocked when he asked, 'Have you ever had a lover?' I heard you say without hesitation, 'No!' The curious moments mingled into the late afternoon with only a promise to read the next manuscript."

Eighteen

"Purple, I just want to stop writing and leave it to other designers of feelings."

"Sport, that doesn't sound like you. Get yourself ready for today, meeting your family for lunch and really immerse yourself in their happy vacation plans. This will help you define what you really want for your own future vacation!"

"Okay, Purple you are better at tracking my emotions than what I can describe. Thanks. Maybe you should be writing this book?"

"Whee, you just landed on a softer lining of my purple bathrobe!"

"Well, the phone rang, and a dental appointment is made for June. Will that be another inside look without wisdom teeth?"

Nineteen

"Sport, you said wisdom teeth, and I know you had those out years ago, but sometimes you don't recognize that wisdom should stick around. You just haven't recognized that I'm so upset hanging around and watching you search for your bearings on who just has become a serious tissue-thin love on a piece of paper."

"Purple, I'm so sorry that this new adventure has made you feel lost too. I'll get a grip on this mystery which may never be solved. So, don't pout and feel neglected."

"Sport, I'm hanging on in a mesmerized state that you haven't moved in your final editing review of *The Peppermint Cottage*! You seem so content in having found our search complete."

"Sorry, Purple, I neglected you during my transitory reading of a book filled with wonder, searching and love. Emotions swirl from inside to out and float like mist that will evaporate. It's like rereading a novelette and being so passionately involved with the characters that it leaves time for a power nap to bank energy. I can't even indulge in that little retreat, because the doorbell sounded. It is the repair man, and the ceiling will soon have its fresh face lift. That's it! I just experienced a lift-off thinking of writing another novelette that begins with a mystery to solve. What do you think, Purple?"

"Count me in!"

Twenty

"Dear Purple, you have such a warm and snug way of comforting my doubting self. Your strength and dedication to keeping me on track are so appreciated. I awoke with a seed of doubt that had to be discarded. You helped with your long arms of encouragement. Thank you! You already sense the importance of that little note, now framed, that is a part of our life now. It has been delicately given the prominence of coming to the computer screen of a new article. Words aren't counted in this life-fulfilling search to find the writer. I hope you understand and just keep me safe in a little cocoon waiting to emerge as a summertime-in-flight butterfly. Dear Purple, you do understand! Why is this shell-covering-itching to be released?

Purple, these are intriguing thoughts, but we can't miss our own little moments when you are so comforting. I awoke to a crashing sound and shuddered who might be entering the patio gate. I listened in pure shock, because everyone I know always calls before unlatching the gate. It banged again, and you afforded me bravery extended by your warmth and arms of reassurance. We went down the long stairway, and the window witnessed our stare of surprise. The gate latch was free to fly back and forth. The wind was so powerful that it gave us a crack of its own mind. Well I'm glad my presence is a need be.

"Oh my, yes, don't ever get put out with pouts of my forgetting to tell you these little secrets that don't even hit the notebooks. It's a cold rainy day, but it has been warmed to a friendly springtime smile when our publisher sent the first navigational plan for our book. This morning, I felt like I was swimming in an ocean of doubt without a life preserver. I know that you also don't like cold water dunks."

"Now you are getting a better picture of me in my age-related condition, and I don't mean you! I've been hanging around for so long really unappreciated, so I'm coming alive to express that silent part of me!"

"I love your expressing that we work together in such a great companionship. Please don't ever wear out and leave me with a little pile of purple threads in a closet corner!"

Twenty-One

"Sport, you are so funny when you have only less than fifteen minutes to shower and dress before the doorbell rings. You took a minute-and-a-half shower, took two minutes to dry off and then hit the deodorant can. You raced for the undies and then got your foot caught in the tug-of-war legging. Threw on a hair brush to the hair do, then hit the lipstick with two quick smears for upper and lower lips. I wasn't there to see if you smiled, as you opened the door in the next second."

"Well, success! But the printer and computer are on halfway terms, and there exists a serious threat that a new printer may have to become a new family member. Purple, that's my homework while the kids are on their fantasy Caribbean cruise. I've got more breathing and searching to do.

"Okay, Purple, while you adjust your listening skills, I'm opening the windows to let this February Caribbean breeze swirl past the rippling tablecloth. This southern luxury could be a prelude to spring if the northern exposure of winter winds doesn't push it away. Along the way past the patio planter, there were four little purple faces with tiny golden centers waiting. These were tenderly picked and placed in a tiny little Jamestown-green-hand-blown vase. Little treasures adding to the much sought-after contentment. We'll have to hold this gift for memory keeping if a snow flake escapes any high-flung clouds. I just want to pack you up and take you for unmapped disclosure. Okay, your bosom buddy is a hopeless romantic who was showered with dreamlike pictures of a floating states room. Yes, room for you too!"

Twenty-Two

"Sport, good grief, I can't keep up with you, let alone understand your everyday living. Do you realize that you just took out the dried clothes, threw these on the sofa and raced to our dialogue? And before that, you didn't finish your French toast for lunch. You stopped with six pieces left on your plate. Why?"

"Well, Purple, at the start of feeling you have had enough, just stop!"

"Hmmm. Then do you mean that your taste changes as you pulled out a few vinegar and salt potato chips to finish off lunch?"

"The satisfying taste of salt and vinegar adds flavor dimension. I just read that they think that salt may be considered as helping to kill cancer. I don't know, it but sure was a good taste fix."

"You always get me in a fix too! You just wiped your salty fingers on right side of my pocket and didn't even give it a gentle touch!"

Okay, Purple I'm just a little messy, but it blended into your soft fabric and doesn't show."

"Yeah, you just hit the remote and flashed past the dog show, and I wanted to watch! The dogs get petted and are not given rough brush offs."

"Purple are you complaining? Maybe we need to think about having another purple bathrobe stationed on your wish list."

"That's a whopping great idea, and I wonder if one size fits all? And what about the slipper size too?"

"Ok, now, calm your blood pressure while I proceed to get a blood test for A1C. I hate going alone, but, Purple, you can't go along."

Twenty-Three

"Sport, this must be turning into a purple bathrobe day. It's going on 1:45 p.m. and you were still snug in my company. Then the phone rang, and you caught it on the first ring. It was a big thank you from your Michigan sister in her snowy world of ice on the roadway. I am sure glad you two can laugh and have so much fun planning the seating new room arrangements. I love to feel you laughing; it means that you are on another happy adventure. Yes, go fix your misspelled lettering, but she loved the letter she found in her mailbox."

"Purple, sister had taken her snow shovel to crack through the snow and ice to get to the letter this morning. Plus, did you hear that I told her about our escapade of the front gate banging its greeting with the winter wind? And the story about dumping the laundry on the sofa, but she wanted to know more about the mystery yellow paper with the most beautiful written thoughts. So far, so good! She's a great one to run ideas across the mountainous miles and give ideas of encouragement."

"You mean I don't give you enough encouragement?"

"Hey, don't get discouraged! We are an inseparable combination, especially on rainy days."

Twenty-Four

"Hurry up, Sport, and catch that funny thought as you dash into the shower!"

"Purple, do you know how can you scrub off the lazy back side of yourself and get a clean sweep on thoughts? Just take first a little undie and in a water-saver moment, add a little soap to the hand and squeeze that job into a fresh water rinse too. After this quick soak, scrub and toweling effort, wipe down the shower stall which was missed yesterday in that one-and-half minute hurry. Throw the towel into the next washer tub, and race for the guest bathroom scales.

"Quick check the scale measure and find that extra potato chip may have helped to add a little micro-tabulation, but the heavier inhibition may be revealed from the minds' own memory. On a roofing day, remember the sudden shock of a man looking in our second story window while we were together, robe and me? He was finishing the last touches of attaching a roofing nail, but it sure nailed this into my photo memory. How can we get the windows washed and, also, clean out that memory? I'll just have to shrug that one off!"

Twenty-Five

"Well, to get rid of the jitters, the wardrobe supplied an ample set of choices. The brown micro-suede slacks spoke up with, 'Do these fit?' Of course, these fit, but there seems too much fabric to encase the belt. But that extra potato chip won't show. I always look at the labels not to see what unknown company supplied these items but to find where the back should be found. So, a dark aqua turtle neck sweater got into shape, and, no, that's not hiding my thoughts like a turtle or ostrich. I'm going out, and, Purple, you can't go along. This everyday living is just what readers are missing in their own maxi-busy lives. They need to realize that comedy is reigning right along in the very boots we all wear. I leave my boots and shoes but bring the socks upstairs. Last night, we met a man on a television show, and his name is Sox. That's because he is so generous with this life style that he gives the homeless socks, the kind that can be worn."

Twenty-Six

"Purple, have you ever heard the expression, 'Be a good egg!'"

"No, I have only heard only about the eggs that are listed as caged or free-range."

"Yes, that's the store-bought kind, but this one is hardboiled and then taken out of its shell, mashed with a fork, added mixed up salt and spices, added mayo and a swizzle of vinegar. Stir this and place on a toasted bagel that already has a waiting layer of butter. Yes, this is my prescription for 'feed a cold and starve a fever!'"

"Well, I did hear you sneeze twice and blow your nose once. I wondered if you were still going out into the rainy day?"

"Oh my, a little oyster shell that is fed to chickens to make their shells hard, and one escaped into my tasty snack. So being a good egg means also being a good sport too. You can have a merit badge since pay raises aren't in the keyboard offing yet.

"Just what does 'free range' mean? It has a lot of strange places and things to think about. But, basically, it means the chicken is not being fit into a cage. Instead, it can roam freely."

"Oh, like your favorite television show when it hits the final stages of bachelors or bachelorettes finding a partner. Does this mean that they will be caged, also?"

"Oh, no! Ha! That's joining in on a venture of laughter, loving and living without walls dividing."

"Sport, we left the egg carton back in the old school days, but you seem to have to find another way to skirt around what and who you really love. I'm happy, too, but the second purple bathrobe would make fine staying company."

Twenty-Seven

"Purple, you just ignited a little-too-early or a too-late fire cracker for me to have to deal with in an old-fashioned manner. Oh, the music adds to this mellow moment of 'climb every mountain until you find your dream.' Yes, Purple, that dream is somewhere, but no one to verify it as mine. All I'm looking for is the one in a billion, when they used to say, one in a million. Then it would be a great big hug of first greeting and then kisses for all the past lost time. Then the hug to become a hug that can be cuddled into a bundling like the old-time-Pennsylvania Dutch used to allow. A feeling of wholeness that puts life into harmony and balance that doesn't tilt. To walk down the street holding hands or arm in arm like the college set used to display. All these longings lost to the workaholics of my past before we met. Purple, you lead me right into strange avenues that create a rare moment of even given thought. No, I'm not going to hide my blushing under the makeup that wasn't put on today. I have no one that I must make up with, only an apology that can't be ever given for not having said, 'I Love You' when I didn't know he was on the demise track. He asked, and I couldn't lie and say those precious words after years of abuse. Oh, dear Purple, can I be forgiven in the high heavens?

"Purple, our relationship is so personal, but that's what people are so afraid to share! Maybe, this is that free range of emotions that the hard-boiled eggs cooked up. I have another pan of three eggs cooking now, and we're back to our everyday refrigerator shelf line up. I wished my refrigerator was as forgiving as the freezer basket. It's neat and always ready to entertain. However, I did break into the little pint of butter pecan ice cream, and I spooned it out of the container without even being a glutton. Funny, 'spooning' used to be a hidden word for kissing. No, Purple, I'm saving my kisses for the mountain summit. It will be that sum of all my hopes, dreams and desires."

"I feel so honored that you brought these feelings out of the wilderness of your life and shared them with me!"

Twenty-Eight

"Your creativity has a spontaneous burst to the point that I can't keep up with you!".

"Oh, dear Purple, you are so observant, but I keep learning about our fun conversations, and do you know that we are really on track with television marvels? The animated characters that are talking have arrived from movies, and now we can talk without criticism. So, Purple, you can feel safe in our chatting. By the way, this is Lent, and the encouragement of doing self-examining of relationships is often done with our Priest, Parish Minister, or our own personal at-one-ment. I hadn't realized this timely expression until today."

Twenty-Nine

"Purple, we just heard our combination for success. We don't ever have to grow up, and that was the creative style of Walt Disney and his Peter Pan. Now, in this season of truth baring, I can tell you why I cried for a week when we moved from Anaheim, California. Those tears were released all the way into the Southeast. If you could feel my grief, it's because I was being offered a contract that I couldn't accept because of being a Navy wife. Yes, I was offered a teaching position as a Master Teacher to work in the Walt Disney Elementary School. That brings up another loss earlier in my life - a Principalship that was offered when I finished my undergraduate work in San Diego County. I guess someone, somewhere cared about my qualifications back then. Thanks, Purple, for being my confidant. I think many people can relate to hard choices. But I have had a wonderful life with many crossed streams. Ha! Once I fell into a New Hampshire river and saved the video camera. Once again, I was all wet!"

"Dear Sport, you are my survivor!"

Thirty

"Purple, why don't we consider having an honest love affair with life? Not an affair between masculine and feminine stars from a universe of their own design, but one of love for a special life filled with emotion! A life where we take a deep gasping breath, because at times it is so exciting that we must call 911 for cardiopulmonary respiration! Did you see that there is a new class sponsored by the Sheriff's office teaching how to give babies CPR? I am so impressed with this sensitivity to those little chests of 1-2-3 press-and-release. God's miracles everyday are happening if we just watch, look, and listen."

"Sport what brought this on?"

"Oh, just being happy in where we are and what we are doing in sharing purpose and fulfillment. You are keeping me warm, and when we return to the lean-back-and-relax chair, the purple afghan will warm my feet. I do get cold feet occasionally when the wild side of life comes bubbling out."

Thirty-One

"Purple, this isn't going to be music to the ears of the short-interest-span individuals unless they are interested in the development of the fast track lane to learning, living and loving. The visual stimulation of commercial watching resulted in my observation that we had just seconds to grasp the whole concept and complexity of the subject matter. A stopwatch of seconds seemed to time one screen subject to another. I would sit and scoop butter pecan ice cream from a little tub, and I found that the ice-tea spoon digging out the chilled yummy was slower than the flash of one commercial to another. The mattress on sale looked luxurious while my ice cream mixed with gooey brownies was making a mess. Then the cosmetics blended into a soft drink, and the color match looked okay. The bigger the commercial name, the longer my attention held. I loved the auto commercials. You know, in the time that we take to edit out an extra letter, we can experience another thought stimulus. That's a wonderful color mix from this world of the manufactured offerings. My degree was in mass communication. But the communication occurs in a world of multipliers. The masses are so filled with multiplicity that going to Mass on Sunday seems like a slow-motion effort. We have got to slow down and enjoy the miracles of simplicity! We need to really look into the eyes of humanity and smile!"

"Is that why you have also been working on studying the manuscript of *Faces*?"

"Yes, Purple, I'm so fascinated with the stories hidden behind the facial lines of people that we meet on the street. I call those their 'story lines.' It might also be fun to see if we can catch the expressions of real people who are hired to be on commercials. Do they display their own emotions and creative imaginations?

"Wow, Purple, there is just time enough to say goodnight and think that a wonderful day of raindrops and heavy clouds has allowed this homebody to relish the time for relaxing. Purple, as I turn off the lights, let's leave on the music of time so that it is ready to refill our senses tomorrow."

Thanks for your time, dear reader, too. This morning I received a gift of words that allowed the flood gates to pour onto these pages today. I send a special thank you to that sender.

Thirty-Two

"Dear Purple Bathrobe, you haven't been left out on my venture through a twelve-hour-fasting period. I have a personal recipe for surviving, and it's without permission for a sugar boost. There's an unspoken commodity called putting the psychological, physiological and spiritual all in the same package of self to find a whole new dimension of success and contentment."

"Whoa, you lost me on those big words!"

"No problem, Purple, because now I'm back home and chilling out with you, holding my physical self in a warmth that I'll label 'contentment.' It's all coming together under a higher-power signature that flew in on the wings of a pair of turtle doves. Now, I've eaten, and I'm going back to hit the restart for the day with a power nap."

Thirty-Three

A great surge of energy can mount before sending a long overdue note across the network. The only premium is in continuing friendships.

"Dear Purple, I know you are hanging out on the wall hook and didn't get to listen to my calling an angel friend and wishing them a 'Happy Valentine's Day'. You do need a little time off to just recuperate from my frequent chatter.

"I've opened the windows and turned up the music to a favorite song, 'The Wind Beneath my Wings.' I'll confess that I have no need to fly away on a swift wind. I'm happy here with little notes that filter in past the skyways and into my comfy shell. Maybe I am related to a hermit crab. But I want to say that I'm done house hunting. Go ahead and laugh."

"Sport, are you sure that this condo has enough space when I finally meet my other matching purple robe? I've been checking, and all the hooks in this bathroom are filled, and the guest room doesn't even have a wall hanger."

"Dear Purple, if your family gets any bigger, we'll just revise and adjust. We would never leave you and the other little purple out in the cold to be homeless. You are so special, and you keep me company! Some homes have names like 'Haven,' but ours would have to have a name like 'Moonlight in Rhapsody.'"

"I know what the moonlight looks like, but what is rhapsody?"

"That's a special feeling that no one can explain except when it is discovered."

Thirty-Four

"Sport, you have absolutely gone too far in deciding to send a g-mail closing to your publisher without considering me! You woke up and got right out of bed and marched to the screen like an Olympic skater. We've been way out ahead of the other contestants for your publisher's attention.

"You dared to think about closing out our heady conversations and didn't even consult my thoughts and feelings. I saw what you thought, that you would quickly delete this on your send button. Surprise! He had gotten a moment to read it before closing out his day of vast communications. Glad you recognized that I have a big part in this sharing. You have taught me so much and I'm not ready to graduate onto your coffee table collection."

"Okay, Purple, you win with your warm charm and funny way of influencing my life. Did you see the blue ribbon at the bottom of the screen announcing how wordy we have become?"

"Yes, and it made me dream of having won a blue ribbon, or is it a gold medal?"

"Well, Purple I'm going out to heat up a cup of coffee and then go hunt for the long-hand articles that you helped to write."

"You mean that I belong in your family of stories?"

"Yes, and you belong along with a famous person as being my friend forever."

"Wow, you really love me!"

Thirty-Five

"Sport, I saw you looking in the old cold coffee cup before emptying it. You were staring at the center spot, and I know you have never read tea leaves. What were you seeing?"

"Your eagle eye didn't see what looked like a little moon picture I had taken not so long ago."

"Then does that mean you are moonlighting?"

"You have caught humor in the middle of the night, and that just makes you more endearing, thanks Purple. Now, in the morning before we hit the 'To Do List', we'll settle into sharing those hidden notes and salvage a couple of dream clusters."

Thirty-Six

"Purple, there's a vibration that emits from a smile. I sent one when a heavy door was opened by a college gentleman along with my 'thank you'. Another happened while I thumbed through a very large historical book which was a successful Broadway play. A distinguished retired college professor, who is also an author, made several suggestions, and so a quiet marketing of our work reached this pen name. I recommended that he check out several writing groups, and he was delighted. He has published, and he gave a keen ear to our publisher, too. He and his wife love to travel, and a bookstore is a wonderful place to visit before continuing. He asked which of my books I would recommend that he get. I said, 'If you like to travel, then *Time on the Turn* is a great beginning.'"

"Sport, do you suppose sometime our *Purple Bathrobe* will reach a book signing table?"

"Well, just add that to your dream list."

Thirty-Seven

"Purple, I'm just in such a mess!"

"Now, Sport, what can be so serious that you would wake me at 3:00 a.m.? You worked until after midnight editing our manuscript, and here you are in such a new mood. What's going on?"

"Oh, Purple, first, I woke up itching all over, and not even the long-handled-back scratcher with the telescoping rake extended could reach all of my rash. I don't have the three-day measles like when I graduated from high school. I think I have a case of nerves. So, I got up and came to the kitchen, and the overly filled new milk jug had to be opened. Now I know what it means, 'Don't cry over spilled milk!' First, I only wanted a quart, but the grocery store only had gallons in stock. The only space in my refrigerator was on the top shelf. Now I'm restricted from lifting over my head due to an old broken shoulder from another long icy winter. Well, there was no choice but to unscrew the blue cap, and it blew its top all over the freshly-cleaned-stove top. I just had to stand by and watch, and I couldn't lift a hand to mop up the mess! Now I understand that old saying about spilt milk perfectly!"

"My mother taught me that saying, too."

"Well, while we're going back to the old country days, let me share that there is another saying that I deplore: 'Keep on crying, and I'll give you something to cry about!' Purple, that meant I had been mischievous and had gotten on Mother's nerves. I always tried to stop short of getting another paddling."

"You mentioned that you now have a rash itching from nerves. How can you explain that?"

"Purple, yesterday I was hurrying and forgot to put on my gold sapphire ring. It happened that I met three men with brief words when they saw my left hand was running on empty. I think this is a hormone rash."

"Sport, you did look neatly put together."

"Well, I'm going back to bed, because I can't tell the difference between commas and periods or life in the single lane. Purple, you always know how to make me feel relaxed, and today when I go out, I'll also remember to put my watch on. By, the way only one of those gentlemen had book-buying potential, and his third finger was encrusted in rings. Thanks, Purple, for making me chuckle in the middle of the night before morning hits the stage. My cup of coffee and crackers have gotten chilled. And, on top of that, it's too dark outside to chill out and walk over to the gushing fountain and add to its splashing."

Thirty-Eight

"Purple, did you listen to my sister and me talking for almost an hour? We chatted about grape pie, blueberry pies, ground cherry and elderberry pie, too. Now, 'elder' just doesn't fit in our conversations. Our communicating is a joy springing forth like water from an artesian well. By the way, we had one of those when the country life style was ours.

"Changing the subject, I told her that I like to wear your cozy, comfy robe to keep me warmed up while talking or writing, but she scolded me about injuries! I had told her about you and our conversation about using the sharp-bladed knife in the kitchen and you warning me not to cut my fingers. She was upset that you had not mentioned band aids or that trips to the emergency room were possible. She said cooking in a robe is dangerous. Ha! We don't have any sexy conversations which could make us an R rated book.

"Speaking of books, she really liked the idea of including our conversations under the cover with *Just Call Me Mom*. Sister dear is my verbal editor of ideas, and I keep her phone number handy. I don't call my editor-formatter- publisher, because he has a multitude of devices besides phones keeping him occupied. Purple, I have never been one to ask for permission. My usual style is to just wait."

"Sport, did you ever consider that the sound of your voice is a nice link in the communication cycle that makes it easy for others to approach you?"

"Ouch! Purple, you figuratively stepped on my right big toe, the one the kids at school loved to get close enough to step on. That's nailing a lot of close calls! Purple, you know how to get under my skin, and when I wear the gold ring, it speaks loudly too. Yesterday, I made a little pact with myself to experiment by not wearing that engaged writing ring. Oh, I think perhaps I've already mentioned it, and don't want to take up your time. I'll not repeat a whole conversation surrounding a 75% off hard-cover book filled with art work that is awesome. A chat that made the seven minutes at that book counter 100% an A+ experience."

"Sport do you rank conversations on the scale of one to ten and how much you enjoy people?"

"Purple, you might be right. I love to write, talk, and discover the people who are willing to step forward and be heard. The clock is ticking, and I have another thought to share."

"Who, what, when, where, and why. I hope you'll give me a clue, as we share almost everything."

Thirty-Nine

"Purple, here's a yarn that has long been suspected. My remote just sent me a message that the batteries were running low. I checked, and I'll have to hunt for double A's. But I hope that these will last through Saturday night, just you and me."

"What does yarn mean? I thought you only knitted with yarn to make a sweater or hat."

"Oh, dear, here comes our lesson on words that puzzles our newcomers to the English language from countries across the sea or across borders, too. Yarn is like knitting together a short story into a shareable piece of literary confusion. However, this brings todays

93

enlightenment into broad view. I was waiting in line to cash a little check, and the wait was getting longer, and the time came to find out why. A pretty lady, put together well with wavy long dark hair, was trying to explain her needs at the teller's window. I really like the word 'Teller' in this case, as it helps to explain how our language, alien to this lady, was a mountain difficult to work through. In retrospect, recently, this has been the case in several grocery lines, when all I needed was to pay for simple purchases like three lotion bottles of creamy delight. So, in discovering the reason behind the wait, I came to the awareness that communication is a vital function in the living and learning process of everyone. I've taught English as a second language, and, maybe, it's time to get another license to prove it. In our society, there always seems to be a need for licenses. That idea never quite gets placed before my pen. Talking and writing about our societal needs may help us all to gain a new edge on patience. Bravo! Maybe I do need to go back to school. Guess what I'll study, Purple?"

"Well, thank heavens you aren't going to be a lingerie or dress department buyer!"

"Oh, my Aunt was one that held big department store names as a buyer in New York. That's the one my mother said should have had me as her daughter!"

"Now, I know how you inherited an eye for shopping and a penchant for storing up adventures. You have a heart for the open road, escalators, and electronic doors. May I accompany you, Sport, and extend my arm of support?"

Forty

"Sport, you should have a gold star for waiting to open a Christmas present from dear friends. Why did you wait so long, when it's already after the holidays and Valentine's Day, too?"

"Purple, these dear friends and I were going to have a birthday treat spent together, but it all got delayed by flying snow and accompanying flu. Tomorrow, we are going to meet at a lovely

94

tourist coffee shop and have desserts to die for. Their heavy box came with a gold-star notecard. The item turned out to be an antique oval crystal bowl that could hold a huge banana split to serve us all!"

"Do you think you could plan a pajama party, and I could be invited?"

"Purple, you are so sweet, but I've never really had a pajama party in mixed company."

"Oh! I thought you might invite the other purple bathrobe!"

"Sorry, Purple, we don't have that on our calendar radar."

"I know about your calendar, but what does radar mean?"

"Well, Purple, it a highly sensitive device that measures waves of objects, and purple threads just wouldn't fit the scope. I do know about CIC, and I'm not going to try to explain the intelligence of *that* creative sightseeing. Let's close our eyes and say, 'Goodnight!'"

"Sport, for goodness sakes, I just heard you see-sawing the towel in a hurried drying after the shower. Then a swish, and over the top of the door came a white wash cloth right that zoomed past me. I threw up that 'hello' arm and kept it from dropping into the open commode. Aren't you glad I saved that from over-consumption?"

"Sorry, Purple, I've neglected you. I've been hung up on overlooked writing mistakes. We can't talk now. I have an important appointment shortly."

"What kind?"

"We will have to discuss sugar talk later."

"Oh, do you mean sweet talk, those sugary little words of endearment?"

"Dear Purple, you are so bright on such a gloomy and cloudy day. Thanks!"

Forty-One

"Sport, you were quiet as you stopped reading our manuscript for editing, and you walked over and closed the front shutters on the windows. You blinked in surprise that a tiny bird had left its hiding place beneath our view. Then you walked in and picked up the big pillow that was hiding a portrait that you had taken a long time ago. Why do you keep it hidden from daylight viewing?"

"Purple, is it because my inner photo joy doesn't want the world to know who, when, where or why?"

"Will you tell me?"

"Nope! That smiling picture is like the original portrait that my daughter drew of Dr. Albert Schweitzer. That huge portrait is very heavy, and it doesn't like to be hung just anywhere. It will fall off the wall without his batting his following eyes. It's an amazing fete, and the one picture beside my bed is there to protect dreams and just not ever to be hung on a gallery wall."

"Ahhhh...won't you tell me more?"

"No, Purple, that's my private secret. You see, if our little chatting time goes beyond our patio wall, it wouldn't be any secret."

"It's funny that you have been able to chat with eleven thousand, two hundred sixty- four words and roll along gracefully without a smidgen who this might be!"

Forty-Two

"Why are you heating the oven to 400 degrees when you haven't been even near the kitchen since coming home from entertaining friends for their birthday desserts? First, what are you going to bake? And second, what was your favorite dessert selection this afternoon?"

"Well, eating dessert before a Banquet-brand-frozen-beef-pot-pie dinner was just the best! I chose the Hummingbird Pound Cake, and it really flew off my little square china plate. The coffee shop at a favorite hotel tourist spot wasn't busy, and we three had the best time catching up on life in our ordinary lanes. They are such awesome professionals that catching their calendar of time off the road is undeniably special. I just turned the local nightly news on, and my guests may have missed the starting lineup for the Daytona race or the Olympics in South Korea. Should I send an email to apologize for this interruption from their watching this afternoon?"

"Sport, they could have said, 'Let's just hold off another weekend for you.' I can tell you don't cook with our time out."

"The oven sounded that it is ready for the made-from-scratch beef pie. That terminology is why I chose that advertising description. We rarely ever hear 'made from scratch!'"

"Why did you choose beef over chicken pot pie on yesterday's shopping spree?"

"Purple, you make me laugh, but I chose beef because we've had so much beefing throughout the media circuits that I thought baking might not be half-baked but, instead, might have time to be finished off."

"Ha! Sport, will there be any leftovers?"

"Purple, you are a gem to ask, and I can say that I freeze leftovers. You would be great at attending a critiquing session."

"I can tell you don't cook with gas! Just be careful when you plug in a new electric floor lamp. By the way, I like the lamp in the bathroom that has a dim, bright and brighter touch in its lighting. I think that is a pretty mood swing."

"Purple, where did you learn about moods?"

"Well, I saw a milk advertisement where cows moo, and I thought it might be okay to misspell and catch your editor off guard!"

"Now, Purple, it may be time for you to hit the wall hook."

"You mean that I can't make you laugh?"

"Okay, you did add a silly streak to my little hidden word signals. Speaking of silly, I heard a comment about a birthday gift of several lovely silk blouses. One recipient said, 'It made me feel kinda' silly!' Was she afraid to say sexy?"

Forty-Three

"Sport, how can I chide and cheer for you all in the same salad bowl? You bought a 'grater', and you have just grated fresh celery, carrot and the most beautiful radish over the top of your salad. Do be careful, and don't get your fingers cut in that item that didn't even give directions of how to use. Plus, are you going to become a vegetarian? I think so, by the looks of that salad splashed with balsamic vinegar dressing! Why do they call that bottled-up liquid, 'dressing?' I thought that was only for dressing gowns."

"Dear Purple, we do need to sit down and discuss the various household tools and room dividers. By the way, can you wrap your head around saying, 'Cheese' when a picture is taken? Try that one for thought while I have dinner of beef pot pie and mixed salad."

Forty-Four

"Sport, what are you looking at, peering from your bowl holding spoon and cereal? Your eyes are raised to the center triad window, and you are motionless."

"Purple, I looked for a bright and shining star before going to bed, but I didn't make any wishes. The time of this opening day is very early, but she has risen early too. That's our planet, Venus, with such a steadfast eye on the spinning earth. I haven't done a lot of planet study to know the scale of planets from smallest to largest in our orbital family. I can't teach you much astronomy tonight, but go ahead and admire these luminescent marvels when they appear before us. Just follow my eyes."

"Well, you do keep your sights high, and now this sister planet has orbited out of sight."

"Yes, and it's much too cold to go star gazing this morning - plus, did you know that today is a holiday? Today is President's Day, a time to give at least give a token of thought to the contributions of our honored leaders across the decades."

"Do these heads of state belong to any Alumni Days? I just noticed that you have saved that flyer on the sewing table."

"My goodness, Purple, you are keeping an observant and sharp eye on my calendar of events on my dream road. Let's just appreciate the contributions that have paved the way for the Presidents' Day to fit into the classroom history pages. I still love the recognition that we can give, thinking that history has a 'his-story.' I wonder if anyone ever saw Venus from the Rotunda?"

"What's a rotunda?"

"Well, I think of it as a big, high dome-shaped ceiling that makes you want to see a Michelangelo painting."

"Can we go to the library today, or will it be closed?"

"Purple, you just sculpted a solidly marble idea, and, if so, we can always visit our favorite bookstore for bound-together stories and paintings of the world at large. Right now, let's allow the seconds and minutes to climb past three o'clock. Venus, you and me! Let's thank the Lord for giving us these little insightful thoughts and feelings to secure the day ahead."

Forty-Five

"Purple, I'm so sorry that I dragged you out into the mist and raindrops to take a picture. From our breakfast seat, you saw me totally enthralled with the view of tiny blossoms forming. I even wrote a note to my editor and then went to take a proof-positive picture. When you and I arrived at the twiglet tree by our pond, I discovered that fake viewing had taken place. The tiny 'blossoms' turned out to be fungi growing in the full bark."

"Well I'm glad you tried to rectify the false hope of spring happening here in mid-February. That's my dreamer in full gear, and nothing stops your optimism!"

"Purple, I'm sorry!"

Forty-Six

"Purple, you were listening when I was saying a little prayer. I'm learning not to give the Lord a big list of the ailments and needs for healing. You felt me chill and subsequently hit a wave of hot-flashing warmth. No, not like hot flash. I'm speaking of the kind that sweeps by leaving a trail of warm air, like the cardinal that raced past my doorway. Next came encouragement in the beauty of words sent through the fog to light upon my computer screen to lift my aching heart."

"Yes, and I saw the prescription labeled, 'Relax'."

Forty-Seven

"The keyboard of recall says, 'Three hours since you visited this site!' Well, Purple, we have another eagle eye on our whereabouts! And this goes along with the music playing the soothing notes of understanding. It's amazing that my favorite songs keep slipping into ear awareness and emptying the channels of silence.

"Now *there's* a new avenue of journeying thought that might be relevant to our plateau of understanding. Our generations, of which so many have been given a label, have raced by us, but each forgotten generation is sending a message of importance! Maybe it's the 'Me Generation' that needs to be explored? Purple, let's just keep this one name in focus today. The 'Me Generation' has been ignored, thanks to the shoving 'busy-ness' of personal and professional living these days. What irony!"

Forty-Eight

"Purple, let's move slowly like slippers on the carpet and allow thoughts to accompany the musical notes of awareness. Could this be our day to add the romanticism that is often unexpressed? I think romanticism swells within all hearts. Has memory become enshrouded in doubt? It's amazing - I left out 'u' in spelling 'doubt.' Thanks, spellcheck."

"Sport, you just dug up a chuckle from inside my wrapped-up folds. Where are you heading now?"

"Well, the fog has lifted, and the blood pressure has kept a steady keel, but the glucose has been a culprit. So, we'll take some of the glucose and put in a little sweet talk. Haha! Getting a handle on the *me* within, I realize that we all need to take a personal test of our own making. This doesn't require multiple choices; rather, honest evaluation of ourselves on the quotient called 'Happiness.' With a slip of a fingertip, misspelling garnered an unsatisfactory rating on a report card. Guess we had all better be required to take a time out in detention hall, now and then! We all have some lessons in learning to distinguish personal and professional things! This author isn't going to get into the specifics, because we all have our own ladders. Today, I'll just give myself credit for trying! And I hope you noticed the word 'crying' wasn't even allowed a tear drop. Just get up the courage to tell your dear ones your feelings like, 'I love you!'"

"Sport, has your heartbeat returned to normal from too-slow-for-comfort?"

(Purple bathrobe got the last word. There's a possibility that Purple Bathrobe will speak up again in the future!).

Forty-Nine

"Sport, why are you eating ice cream with a long-handled-ice-tea spoon?"

"Well, it just fit my mood to take little scoops and feel the fresh cold chill slowly slip across my tongue and down my throat. Also, the word, 'ice,' with tea and cream seemed to make summertime come a little closer in all choices of flavors!"

"Why did you pick a quart of butter pecan ice cream from the grocery freezer?"

"Well, that comes from a long tradition of the whole family having this as a favorite."

"Do you suppose the other purple bathrobe's owner enjoys that too?"

"Purple, you have such an imagination when it's almost bedtime and slowing down is the moment when desserts fit the closing of day. Today has melted like the little remaining scoops in the stem-shaped-crystal-sherbet dish. We should savor each day and whatever has made it a special treat. Purple, thank you for sharing this day and these special moments with me to reflect on enjoying treasures of time."

"How do you mean, 'treasure?'"

"It's that unexplained satisfaction and contentment that can't be described until it becomes a miracle of feeling. Goodnight, dear Purple."

"Ice cream sure is powerful! Goodnight, Sport, I love you!"

Fifty

"Sport, what prompted you to jump out of bed and race to our computer desk and begin composing?"

"Oh, Purple, this is so marvelous! From the depths of dream sleep came blending of fragments as if from an electric mixer to form a short story. I'm here right now to write that dream in whole-story form on my lit screen, and the composing keeps coming like the internet explorer that I joined before going to bed. It almost seemed like the password had allowed it to move into reality to sit on the counter top here in the kitchen. A totally unbelievable and exciting event from surrealism into reality, or was it a prompt? Because from the tiptop of brain came the laptop of promise. Now it's apparent that to purchase a laptop for the very first time means that we'll be taking a trip back into the heartland of our Americana."

"Wow! Do you think that the storm outside which is a swirling March madness called 'Riley' woke you up to record this dream?"

"Maybe, Purple, and this is so exciting that I must again repeat: From tip top to lap top, we have just recorded our dream for a new sales slip. We will have to research discounts for seniors and where to get the best price. This has been a priceless experience that proves dreams can come true, born in the mind and completed in mechanical process."

"Go ahead and raise your cup of blessings!"

"Purple, it's funny you said that, because the cup is from a bank account. No telling how far this will reach. In totality, our thirteen minutes have been exhilarating."

"Whew, that big word just blew over me with a big blast! Please explain!"

"No, Purple, it's enough to have shared what I did. Now it's time to slip back into bedtime dreamland. Editing in the morning will be another awakening, followed by going out to buy another ink cartridge to prove this really is waiting for us to share with our publisher."

"Do you think he will laugh, chuckle or hit the road flying?"

103

Fifty-One

"Hi, Sport, so glad you grabbed me after that hot shower. I want to know if I can go along today?"

"Oh, Purple it's so hard to tell you like I used to do with my little girls: Not today!"

"Why not?"

"Well, it's a trip with many little detours."

"What's a detour?"

"Well, that's little tours in and out and all around the town."

"You mean people don't like purple?"

Oh, no, that's not it! You don't have big enough pockets to put in an onion and uncooked pizza for the kids returning from their cruising vacation."

"Would I get smelly? That's a thought! By the way, you startled last night when sounds went bump, why?"

"Oh my, here we go again. The sound was like someone pounding on our front door, and I knew it was fortified with double locks. This morning I discovered that I had heard chairs overturning on the club house deck near us."

"Does 'club house' mean that people get clubbed when they use it, and the chairs fall over?"

"Purple, we need another serious talk, but don't ever be afraid of the wind in its wild knocking. In the Midwest, people have storm cellars for refuge from wind, or they squat down in their bathtubs."

"Oh, like getting ready for a community bath?"

"Hey, will you stop making me laugh and wanting to keep rubbing elbows with the word, 'structures'?"

104

"What's a structure?"

"I'm going to stand you in the corner and race out to feed the vacationers' kitties now."

"Oh, you mean those critters that have nails that scratch. Are they good back scratchers?"

"Purple, I'll be back in a few hours. We'll curl up and watch the Oscars then."

Fifty-Two

"Well, you really did remember your promise about our watching the 90th Oscar presentations."

"Yes, Purple, I always try to keep promises, but first I must say that if you thought I might stand you up, I'm sorry. While surfing the channels, I landed on the PBS station, and it was featuring a special from the Florence Concert Hall. I heard the most beautiful Italian voices of three talented young men with baritone and tenor delivery. The music provided vibrations of magic. If I had to choose between attending the Oscars or that Italian Opera, I'd pick the Opera vocalists and their songs of 'Maria' and 'I Did It My Way.' Music erases barriers of the mind, and the ear feels these pulsations in harmony and flowing freedom."

"Sport, you really do get carried away!"

"Here's for another little amusing wardrobe. In my closet is a beautiful black linen gown with gold-threaded designs, and I'd wear it to a concert. I don't care that it is an elegant Turkish house dress that I bought at a kiosk years ago. To me, it's good for a night on the town."

"Do they still make purple jumpsuits with gold trim?"

"Ok, let's go back to the Oscars after our brief intermission."

"I want to see the black-tie gentlemen and ladies in their designer riggings."

"Purple, why did you say the ladies in their riggings?"

"Well, I noticed the other day on television that some ships have sails, and they call those 'riggings.' Just thought that described the high-priced dresses."

"Purple!

Fifty-Three

"Oh, Purple! I'm sorry that I threw the wet shower cap onto your neckline and didn't even notice you wince in dismay!"

"What does 'wince' mean? I tried to hide my showered feelings."

"Well, 'wince' isn't a word we often use, but it means showing an expression of pain, sometimes accompanied by a little ducking for cover."

"Oh!"

"I've got to rush out and clear up a big list of run-around errands. I hope that the English pink magnolia will have burst forth its buds into this beautiful sunny day. I'll bring you a picture if it is photo ready. Bye for now!"

Fifty-Four

"Sport, your late lunch has brought me to sit up and take notice. I just wanted to let you know that I'm learning more everyday about your antics. The latest discovery is that I know what the term 'potato chips' means, especially when I see you mashing the chips. You have chips flying like the wood cutters' chips for carving a pipe."

"Oh, dear Purple, you do make me so proud of your observations, but these are for dredging chicken tenders in the chip flakes and baking for dinner. May I sit with you and tell you about yesterday?"

"You seemed all wrapped up like a fast food advertisement with stuffing oozing out, but without any aroma."

'Purple, you seem to have such a hunger for learning! That kind of wrap isn't the kind that I find wrapped around you."

"Well, I'm glad about it, because you don't have any bibs to help keep me neat."

Fifty-Five

"Dear Purple, let's chill out for a little while. We just digested four portions of a book of winging thoughts. It feels good to have finished it, and, truly, I hope there might be a sequel to add to the joy provided. Now the lists of today are waiting. The box of crackers promised that each one held one hour of energy. I've eaten two, and, watching the clock, I am prepared to do the most important duties during that frame of promise. So, I'm going to gently place you on the end of the bed to wait for nighttime comfort and shelter."

"Thanks, Sport, so glad you didn't throw me on a hook. I really have a hang-up about comfort. Have fun, and I wish I could see your delight when the perfect pink magnolia comes to roost on your digital setting."

"Ah, Purple, forgive me. The phone rang, and the gentleman said, 'I'm sorry, I have the wrong number.' He had a heavy voice, and not one of intrigue. Speaking of voices, in the memory cells of recall, one can find beautiful introductions from the sender to receiver. Think about those voice tones that are so lasting! Now, Purple, we should fit 'puzzle' into a list of things to be completed right now!"

Fifty-Six

"Hurry up, Sport, you are on that two-hour-proof-of-purchase energy dividend. But for goodness' sake, I've got a big question to ask first. I saw on television that a hazardous material team was called to hose down a chemical spill, and they hosed down the area. Why did you toss your hose in the sink and continue to rub it down?"

"Well, Purple, when I put the hose on, it had a runaway thread which left a big gaping hole, so, being on a budget, I just use it to remove the soap and toothpaste in the sink."

"Oh, then it was a hose-down, after all!"

"Purple, you are worth all the time to answer your clever questions and listen to your silly thoughts. I just enjoy you so much."

"Ditto!"

Fifty-Seven

"Sport, I watched you spoon down another sherbet glass of pecan ice cream, and I'm so grateful you didn't let it dribble on me. You usually have toast crumbs caught in my lapels and forget to shake them off."

"Sorry, Purple if you think I'm crummy."

"Oh, no, not now. That could be classed as an 'NNN' code. (No, Not Now). By the way, on your way to bed, I saw you take out two band-aids, pull these apart and begin to doctor your left big toe and heel. Why? What are these doing on your left foot?" Does that mean the left foot doesn't want to be left out?"

"Purple, you can be so inquisitive in the middle of my finally hitting the hay."

"What does 'hitting the hay' mean?"

"Purple, that's an old-timey expression for going to bed. Maybe these toes even got caught in a hayride while exchanging kisses. I really don't know. I only went to one taffy pull. Taffy gets in your teeth, and sticky kisses might have been hard to explain and pull apart. Purple, just look, we hit a crazy bone, and it's hard to stop the crafting and get back into the bed."

"What in the world is a crazy bone?"

"Here we go! It's that elbow that gets a strong bump and it tingles all the way to your toes."

"Then, that's why you must have hurt that big toe."

"No, it's from a dry crack and not a wise crack like you are pulling this late at night."

"Oh! You just changed the clocks last night to springing ahead, and I haven't caught up yet! NNN!"

Fifty-Eight

"Sport, I just saw you pull out a strip of scotch tape and wind it around that loose band aid. I know you aren't a stripper, but does that explain you having Scotch and Irish genes running around in your brain cells?"

"I think we need to check to see if you would qualify for the Mensa test, Purple."

"Does that mean they would stick me with a needle and draw my threads out in a string? I really don't want to be at loose ends. Oh, then, too, I saw you turn the lights off twice in the last little while. I heard you tell a story once of a little girl standing at the blackboard, trying to learn how to work out a math problem. You worked with her patiently, silently awaiting her, and, suddenly, she yelled, 'I've got it!'"

"And the neon bulbs above in the ceiling came on. Was that a short circuit!"

"Sport, you have me all wound up! Just one more question: Why do you get silly late at night?" Your circuits seem to rev up like a search engine."

"Dear Purple, maybe we are contagious when there is so much to be happy about."

"Yeah, do you suppose we have made a few readers laugh?"

Fifty-Nine

Breaking news during this short commercial break from watching the beginning of "Skylar": The name is so appropriate in this latest snow storm across the Mid-Atlantic and into New England. The drip-drops of rain soon developed into the geometric shapes of snowflakes that produced the cotton puffs in gusto. I've got to go and get Purple and let her see what shapes of diagonal wind-sweeps look like under the straight line of snow pouring down. However, before our little warm fuzzy questioner arrives on the scene, we must remember something with deep respect. The South used to be known as the King of Cotton. I have a little recall to share:

On a sunny hot day, cotton was being picked and dumped into a truck for sending off to a mill. The man in charge of this expensive commodity was packing it down, and his method was jumping up and down. The cotton was flying above his head, and it looked like a snow storm had overtaken the calendar again. No camera caught this far flung expression of cottony surprise. Did he feel the freedom flying past his feet and into the sky? Just another "Skylar". Bales of fun unleashed!

Sixty

"Dear Purple, I have just figured out a recipe for getting rid of taxing numbers floating around in my brain."

"Well, I noticed that you were all wound up in my cozy presence but had a headache."

"Yup, I decided after a snack and working through the tax accounting that the headache would have to go! I went off to pile pillows around my busy brain and rest in this comfort and your concern. So, in letting all these revisions unwind from loops in my brain, I became clear enough to realize something: People want to find peace and warm fuzzy reassurance that the world is a good place, so we are going to propose to our editor and publisher a new attachment. Let's go for wild and add our *Purple Bathrobe* to the *Just Call Me Mom* book release!"

"Sport, now you are cooking! The chicken noodle soup in the crock pot is bubbling, and I can see that your noodle is doing great. And I see you are back in exactly two hours, but did you remember to button up your form-fit blouse when you dashed past me? Plus, I noticed that you got your mascara on crooked, and a New York Institute of modeling wouldn't have agreed with me more."

"How did you find out about that?"

"Well, I don't get nosey, but I always figure that there's a reason behind you putting makeup on even when we are at home."

"Dear Purple, you would make a great feminine valet, and would you like to start your own business?"

"Okay now you think I should mind my own business!"

"Well, that exercise in being a model came when the girls were in their 'Teen Queen' years, and I was their mom, but I didn't get a certificate. I could talk, smile and learn about their makeup tips, but I didn't weave and sway down the runway in their elegant format. Just fun, and today I relapsed into memories despite crooked eye brows. Haha!"

Sixty-One

"Dear Purple, I've been chasing you all over this keyboard, and the in-and-off pages are scaring me. I just hope we haven't lost any of these to the Urgent Care Center."

111

"Well, I saw you give an extra blink when, in opening the screen, the Christmas book with the gold cover popped up with flickering edges."

"Yes, Purple, and my thoughts went winging like an angel, like the one who reminds all of us that Christmas can't be forgotten. Maybe that angel has been guarding those pages since it has to wait for the holiday to come rolling in again."

"Nothing that you have composed should be forgotten. I think that computer flickering is a reminder to guard and save everything you write - especially about me!"

Sixty-Two

"Purple, what explains the ad arriving here before our eyes for airline reservations with Aer Lingus to Ireland with a shamrock beckoning? Because earlier I had been looking into this. Does our computer follow us on our little avenues of seeking Twitter news from Wild Cottage Ireland? Lack-of-privacy already discloses that we have 16,314 words in our conversations. What happens when word images hurry past the spelling? Does someone in the software laugh? Whatever is the answer, there is no fright in this field of rising dreams. We just added forty more words, and for us it means catching forty more winks."

"What does forty winks mean?"

"That means it's high time to put these conversations to bed - you, me and the computer. If someone out there is laughing, I hope our fancy footwork of ignoring being invaded in the privacy of our studio hits their funny bone. The music right now is playing a familiar tune of 'Around the world in eighty days', and I'd want more than that for global trekking and gliding through rivers of wonder."

"Yeah, me too!"

Sixty-Three

Dear Readers of *The Purple Bathrobe* and *Just Call Me Mom,* I've struggled with the closing protocol as I try to have an ending with softening thoughts. I've wrestled for hours in the word bank of my mind to find a little closing prayer. This one was taught on bended knee as a tiny child and emblazoned for permanent memory. I choose it for the simplicity of its beauty:

"Now I lay me down to sleep, I pray the Lord my soul to keep, and if I die before I wake, I pray the Lord my soul to take."

Words are powerful, and it is sometimes strange listening to our own lips speaking. Writing, too, entails huge responsibility. I pray that even a few of these lines held together with a strong spine will have provided enjoyment and a few laughs. Remember that life may seem ordinary when it is truly extraordinary. Thank you for our moments spent together.

From Sport, with blessings and love.

"And the Purple Bathrobe, too!"

114

About the Author

Marilyn studied education at Manchester College, earning her BS in Education and then her MA in Mass Communications at Norfolk State University. She completed all but her dissertation in the doctoral program of Education Administration at California Coast University. A retired gifted-students teacher who began her career working at Dr. Albert Schweitzer Elementary School in Anaheim, California, Marilyn next devoted 20 years to teaching in the public-school systems of two Virginia cities. Marilyn has also spent years with her own photography business and philanthropic work. In 2015, she became co-founder of The Writer's Council, an organization serving to encourage aspiring writers to achieve their dreams to become published. One of her proudest recognitions is the magazine profile recognition in "Women of Distinction" in 2016.

The author (as M. J. Scott, USA) believes that naming organizations and achievements is a bat of the eye for readers. Much more important, she believes, is the love communicated through genuine sharing of homespun adventures and word-captures of ordinary life. With her characteristic bubbly personality, Marilyn uses humor to connect with readers. This radiates throughout *The Purple Bathrobe* and underlies the inspirational tribute to motherhood in *Just Call Me Mom.*

This is the sixth book by author, M. J. Scott, USA. Her other volumes include *Journey to Fulfillment, Time on the Turn, Power Steering, Power Steering 2* and the novel, *Sport's Alien Fantasy* co-authored with Daniel Wetta. Learn more about these on the author webpage: M. J. Scott webpage